W9-CSP-833

DIVINE Whispers

Stories that speak to the heart & soul

Chana Weisberg

TARGUM/FELDHEIM

First published 2005
Copyright © 2005 by Chana Weisberg
ISBN 1-56871-368-1

Published by:
TARGUM PRESS, INC.
22700 W. Eleven Mile Rd.
Southfield, MI 48034
E-mail: targum@netvision.net.il
Fax: 888-298-9992
www.targum.com

Distributed by:
FELDHEIM PUBLISHERS
208 Airport Executive Park
Nanuet, NY 10954

Printing plates by Frank, Jerusalem
Printed in Israel by Chish

When G-d entrusted the Torah to the Jewish people, He asked them for a guarantor to ensure that it would be properly observed. They responded: Let the three forefathers be our guarantors. He refused. They said: Let our children be our guarantors. Immediately, He consented and gifted to them the Torah.

(Midrash Tanchuma, Vayigash, ch. 2)

Dedicated to my precious children

Esther, Aharon, Naomi, Shira, Yisroel Pinchas, and Sara Leah

Contents

III. FAITH AND ACCEPTANCE

Preface

Finding Spiritual Meaning in Everyday Living

The chassidic master Rabbi Nachman of Breslov would say:

"Many individuals have fallen into a deep sleep,
a profound spiritual lethargy.
There are those who are in such a deep slumber,
they are not even aware that they are asleep.
The way to awaken and ignite these souls
is through stories."

Several months ago I was flying to Las Vegas from my home in Toronto to deliver a lecture entitled, "Finding Heavenly Meaning in Daily Living." It was a busy period in my personal life since my baby, Sara Leah, was only several months old and it was the first out-of-town invitation I had accepted since she was born. It was also the first time since her birth that I had several hours of uninterrupted time to think, which I hoped to use to reflect on my talk, slated for that evening.

As the plane hit some turbulence in the sky, I thought about how life, too, is turbulent. It is filled with so many ups and downs, good times and bad ones, aggravations and frustrations, as well as successes and triumphs.

How, indeed, are we expected to find "heavenly meaning" in all the mundane – and often irritating – quagmire of daily living?

The plane continued to rise higher and higher. Though I travel quite a bit, I've never become completely accustomed to it. I experience a small tension and queasiness during every flight, just as I never lose fascination with the wonder of liftoff and flying so high above ground.

High up in the sky, I experience freedom and distance from the mundanity and pettiness of daily living. The details of whatever project I'm working on or whatever issues in life are pulling me down – all those situations that I've left behind – for the moment are seen from the distance as I gain a new perspective that will help me deal with it all better when I return in a day or so.

As the plane lifts off into the sky, I watch the huge skyscrapers that illuminate the downtown corridor becoming transformed into tiny matchboxes, powerful trucks and cars becoming as small as crawling ants. From this view, it is impossible not to realize the temporality and smallness of our lives and focus on making each moment count.

I mused that perhaps that's the meaning of finding heavenly meaning in daily living. Taking that step back, pausing from the busyness of our lives, to see, appreciate, listen to, and discover a whole new perspective.

As I came closer to Las Vegas, the snow of our northern winters melted away, and we began flying over mountains and valleys. At one point we passed over the stunning Grand Canyon, and from the plane window I watched the most beautiful, picturesque scenery unfold.

From above, from afar, the view of rich brown deserts and tall, elegant mountains made a gorgeous panorama. Even the few silver clouds in the sky took on a certain aura of heavenly magnificence.

I knew all too well, though, that from below, when living through the parched desert periods of our lives, or when strenuously attempting to climb those slippery mountain slopes of our personal challenges, or even when focusing too closely on one imperfection in the landscape of our day-to-day affairs, the view is not nearly as pretty. Frustration, uncertainty, sadness, or despair sets in, and what could have been picturesque beauty deteriorates into the difficulties of daily living.

The Ba'al Shem Tov teaches that everything a person witnesses or hears should serve him as a lesson on how to serve the Creator. Every event seen or heard is purposeful. Time, energy, intelligence, experiences — all are a springboard for us to develop ourselves into the person we want to become.

Sometimes, though, we get so sidetracked with the details of the events that we neglect to perceive the whole picture that is emerging. Sometimes we focus on the parched, dry sand and miss out on the grandness of the scene.

The Torah is a universal blueprint for our lives, filled with communication from G-d to teach us how to lead more meaningful, purposeful, and spiritual lives. The events, episodes, and stories of our lives are also an ongoing communication to us from G-d. These are the personal messages that are being whispered to each of us.

But it is up to us to take a pause from the busyness of our daily lives, to take a step back — with a heavenly view from above — to hear and reflect on those messages.

Divine Whispers hopes to take you on a virtual plane flight, to take a step away from the situations in your life and discover their deeper, divine message.

Divine Whispers is a book of stories — stories from the past as well as contemporary ones; remarkable or even miraculous stories, as well as those of everyday fare. But, like all the events in our lives, each of the stories in *Divine Whispers* is remarkable in that it teaches a profound lesson on how to view ordinary and extraordinary events. All contain a seed of a profound Torah insight — a G-dly communication to us — from which we can derive essential lessons in our quest to lead more meaningful lives.

Following each section in *Divine Whispers* is a list of "personal journal" questions. Your answers to these questions can provide a way for you to evaluate important areas in your life. Record your answers in your own journal, or just think about these questions as you move through the routine of your day. As you do, you will find that your day progresses with a greater awareness and a deeper, more spiritual perspective.

As you read on, you will smile, cry, laugh out loud, or have shivers run down your spine. Cuddle up with these stories at the end of a difficult day as you celebrate, lament, rejoice, and grieve over both the wondrous and the frustrating encounters of your life. But even more, I hope you let your soul listen to each story's message to experience life more fully and with a greater awareness of G-d, yourself, and the world around you.

Divine Whispers hopes to take you flying, high in the sky. It challenges you to storm the depths of your heart, brain, and soul to discover the divine whispers that beckon to you in all of your life's occurrences and, as you do, transform yourself into the person you truly want to be.

Acknowledgments

The following individuals were instrumental in bringing this book to publication. To all of you, I offer my sincere appreciation.

To Steeles Memorial Chapel, the board of directors and specifically the president, Kenny Bodenstein. Your commitment and dedication to servicing the community and enriching *Yiddishkeit* in Toronto is legendary. Your generous support attests to your sincere appreciation of teaching and spreading Torah values.

To the staff at Targum Press, and in particular Rabbi Moshe Dombey, Miriam Zakon, and my editor, Suri Brand: Your insights, recommendations, and experience in producing this book undoubtedly enhanced it enormously.

To Yanki Tauber, the editor of www.chabad.org weekly magazine, where many of these essays first appeared: Your talent in finding just the right word and polishing every article that chabad.org publishes has left your talented imprint on this book.

To the readers of my columns at chabad.org, *The Jewish Press*, and Aish.com who took the time to write me a short note, letter, or comment: Your feedback provided me with the encouragement to continue writing, and your recommendations have helped to improve these essays.

To my students: Often it was through your questions, or through the classes I was preparing for you, that I tried to bring profound ideas more down-to-earth, using practical examples and stories from life. The result was several stories recorded in this book.

To my in-laws, Rabbi Yankel Weisberg, ע״ה, and תלטי״א, Mrs. Henchie Weisberg, for your constant and unwavering support and encouragement. My father-in-law's recent passing has left a void in our hearts, and it is our sincere hope that we carry on leading our lives with the dedication to Torah that you have unwaveringly demonstrated throughout your life.

To my parents, Rabbi Dovid and Mrs. Batsheva Schochet, for the foundation that you have given me and the encouragement that you continue to give. Several stories within this book are about episodes in your lives. The stories reflect but a small percentage of the values you impart to all of your children through your exemplary lives.

To my beloved children, Esther, Aharon, Naomi, Shira, Yisroel Pinchas, and Sara Leah, as well as to my dear husband, Isser Zalman, for all that you continue to teach me. It is a humbling experience to be both a mother and wife to you, and each day I learn and discover how little I know and how much I must learn. Through all of life's ups and downs, good times and hard ones, having you at my side has been a constant inspiration full of encouragement.

To the Rebbe, many of your teachings and attitudes toward life, faith, and hardships are reflected in the stories of this book. These teachings provide lifegiving waters as we live through these parched desert periods of our lives.

And, finally, to the Master of the universe for all He has and continues to give to me. May we speedily experience the time when the knowledge of Torah will be overflowing "as the waters cover the seabed."

I. You

ON IDENTITY
ON POTENTIAL

The chassidic master Rabbi Shlomo of Karlin said:

"The worst sin is to forget you are a child of G-d,
a prince in the divine royal court.
Being aware of your status prevents you
from taking part in actions
that are beneath your dignity."

On Identity

My Father and the Priest

Almost forty years ago my father, Rabbi Dovid Schochet, was asked to lecture to a group of Jewish and non-Jewish participants in the neighboring city of Buffalo. Reluctant to accept the invitation, my father consulted with his uncle, Rabbi Chodakov, secretary of the Lubavitcher Rebbe, who urged him to do so. My father focused his lecture on the theme of charity, due to its universal application to both Jews and non-Jews.

My father began with the following story:

A wealthy individual who never contributed to charity lived during the time of the Tosfos Yom Tov, a great Jewish sage. After this miser died, the *chevrah kaddisha* (the society responsible for the burial of and performing the rites on the body) felt that he was unworthy of being interred next to any upright and respectable individual and buried him, instead, in the area of the cemetery called "*hekdesh*," reserved for society's outcasts and destitute.

A few days after the funeral, a tumult developed in Cracow. The butcher and baker, two prominent members of the community, who had hitherto been extremely charitable, suddenly stopped distributing their funds. The poor people, who had relied on the benevolent pair for their sustenance, now were in a state of uproar. Emotions ran so high that the matter was finally brought before the Tosfos Yom Tov.

He asked the two why they had so abruptly terminated their worthy acts. They replied:

"In the past, this 'miser' continuously supplied us with funds for charity. He strongly warned us, however, not to disclose our source, since he wanted the great merit of performing the mitzvah in a hidden manner. Now that he is dead, we are no longer able to continue."

Awed by the unassuming "miser's" behavior, the Tosfos Yom Tov requested to be buried next to this humble individual, even though this meant being interred in a disreputable section of the cemetery.

As my father concluded his lecture, a participant from the audience, who happened to be a priest, approached him and requested that he repeat the story. My father did not wish to be seen having a drawn-out dialogue with a priest and therefore arranged a time to meet with the priest the following day in his hotel room. Thinking that the matter would be forgotten, my father was surprised when, at the appointed hour, the priest actually arrived.

In the room, the priest once again pleaded with my father to repeat the story. My father obliged, but was astounded when, after concluding the story a second time, the priest seemed terribly distraught and begged him to repeat it yet again.

By this point, the priest was nervously pacing back and forth across the room. Finally, he divulged the reason for his agitation. He turned to my father and confessed, "Rabbi Schochet, that charitable man in the story was my ancestor."

Skeptical, my father calmed the young man, saying that there was absolutely no connection between him and the story, which had taken place hundreds of years ago. "Furthermore," he told him, "you are not Jewish. This man was a Jew."

The priest looked at my father intently and whispered, "Rabbi, now I have a story to tell you!"

He began by describing his background. He had grown up in the state of Tennessee. His father was a major in the U.S. army during the Second World War. Overseas, in Europe, the major met a Jewish girl and brought her back home as his war bride. No one knew her background. A short time after their marriage, the couple was blessed with a child, whom they devoutly raised in the Catholic tradition. The child grew up and attended a seminary where he eventually trained to become a priest.

In his early adulthood, the priest's mother died prematurely. On her deathbed, she disclosed her secret identity to her completely baffled son. After reciting the Shema prayer, she confessed, "I want you to know that you are Jewish." She informed him of his heritage and that his ancestor was buried next to a great sage called the Tosfos Yom Tov. She then recounted, almost verbatim, the story that my father had told in his lecture.

At the time, the priest imagined that his mother was delirious. Although he felt uneasy by his mother's parting words, it was only a temporary, fleeting emotion. As he got on with his life, he soon forgot the entire episode and lost interest in the subject.

"Rabbi," cried the priest, now in a state of complete emotional upheaval, "you have just repeated my mother's story, detail for detail. You have reminded me of my mother's parting words. I realize now that the story must be true. Yet what am I to do? I am a reputable priest with a large congregation of devoted followers."

My father offered to assist him in any way possible. He emphasized to him, however, that according to Judaism, he was indeed Jewish. He encouraged him to explore his heritage and put him in contact with people in his city who could guide him. With that, the weary, newly found Jew departed.

My father had no future correspondence with this man and heard nothing further from him.

Several years ago, on a visit to Israel, a bearded religious Jew approached my father at the Kotel and wished him, *Shalom aleichem.*

My father didn't recognize the individual and was completely taken aback when the man exclaimed, "Don't you recognize me, Rabbi Schochet? I am the former priest whom you met in Buffalo!" He added, "A Jew is never completely lost from his people."

~ ~

I recently discovered that my father is a direct descendant of the Tosfos Yom Tov. At that auspicious juncture in time, in a hotel lobby in Buffalo, New York, the descendant of the Tosfos Yom Tov met with a descendant of the miser — and miraculously changed the course of destiny.

> ~ *Events in our lives may sometimes seem haphazard. Whether we realize it or not, though, they are leading us to discover our true identity and return to our inner calling.*

Shabbat in Lvov

Lvov, Soviet Union

"Batya, the group is leaving on the train tonight," Rabbi Pinchas Sudak said to his wife. He spoke in a whisper, even though there was no one present in the privacy of their home.

In Soviet Russia of the 1940s, where spies, informers, or the secret police could be hidden in any corner — where it was said that the walls themselves had ears — precaution and secrecy was part of the fabric of their lives. One could never be too careful, and all the more so with the perilous topic at hand.

Batya was well aware of the meaning behind the emphasis in her husband's words and of the potential for hope that they held. The Sudaks were temporarily settled in Lvov, a city near the Polish border. They had chosen this location to plot their getaway from the Soviet Union. They had recently obtained forged documents which would allow them to pose as Polish citizens and board the train crossing the border into freedom.

The group Pinchas was referring to were families of fellow Lubavitcher chassidim who, together with him, had planned this bold escape. Should the group be caught and their papers examined more closely, it would mean immediate imprisonment and most probably a death sentence for each of them. It was a risk, though, which they felt they had to take.

Batya voiced her protest. "But tonight is Friday night, Pinchas."

"It is *pikuach nefesh* (an issue of life and death)," Pinchas answered tersely but decisively.

Batya was well aware that violating the Shabbat was permitted if it involved saving one's life. She knew all too well that this situation would be classified as life-threatening and traveling was unquestionably acceptable.

"Yes, of course," she replied, her voice faltering. "But how can we? After all we've been through to uphold the sanctity of Shabbat and to keep the mitzvot, should we desecrate it now? At this point?

"It is a dangerous trip. We could be paying with our lives," she argued. "How can we undertake it on the holy day of Shabbat? No!" Batya concluded, greater determination now evident in her voice. "We will not travel tonight."

"We'll miss the train and traveling with our group," Pinchas objected. "There may not be another opportunity..."

"No." Batya was adamant. "We will not travel. I will go and tell them."

Before any doubt could seep in and cause her determination to waver, Batya headed rapidly down the steps of her home, toward the front door. In her haste, she missed the last step and landed on the floor, her foot badly twisted. She cried out in pain, and Pinchas was immediately at her side. He helped her to a chair and raised her leg. Within moments the foot ballooned and became a large, swollen mass.

Thus the decision was made for the Sudaks. With Batya's swollen ankle, it would be impossible for them to make the journey.

The Sudaks observed that Shabbat as they did every other one — with as much joy and calm as they could muster. They would not allow any doubt or uncertainty about their future mar the sanctity of the holy day.

It wouldn't be until several days later that the Sudaks learned the fate of the others with whom they had almost departed.

That Friday night, the families in the group boarded the train as scheduled, carrying their false documents and all their worldly possessions. The adult members of the group each breathed a deep sigh of relief as they crossed the Russian-Poland border.

But their relief was short-lived. A new danger awaited them.

A group of armed bandits suddenly attacked the train. The passengers pleaded with the unruly men to spare their lives. "Take all our money and possessions," they implored, "just allow us to live."

The group was fortunate that the bandits seized their belongings but consented not to kill them all. Many hours later, the group finally arrived in their destination in Lodz, Poland. They were thankful to be alive but were penniless and destitute, having lost all of their life's savings.

⇜ ⇝

Back in Lvov, at the close of Shabbat, the Sudaks began making new plans for their escape. They received news that another train had become available and would be departing the following Tuesday night. Batya's foot was by now completely healed, and the Sudaks made the necessary arrangements to board this train.

Batya and Pinchas and their three children arrived uneventfully in Lodz, grateful to have escaped from the Soviet Union and to have successfully completed this part of their journey toward freedom.

Batya's injured foot and the merit of the holy day of Shabbat had saved them from a terrifying and life-threatening ordeal and enabled them to keep their valuables, which would be so vital for their survival in a foreign land. Batya and Pinchas couldn't help but think how true it was that "more than the Jewish people have kept the Shabbat, the Shabbat has kept the Jewish people."

One of the children on that fatefully delayed train ride was my mother, Rebbetzin Batsheva Schochet, the oldest of the three Sudak children. Years later she would serve, together with her husband, as one of the first Chabad emissaries sent to vitalize the Toronto Jewish community. She has devoted her life to what her parents struggled so hard to uphold, helping others to discover the beauty and magic of Shabbat and the Jewish traditions.

⇚ *Following your convictions can involve deep sacrifices. But ultimately we are enriched from those life choices.*

Silent Messages

My father-in-law, Rabbi Yaakov Weisberg, passed away a few months ago, in the closing days of the Jewish month of Elul. The month had always held special meaning for him. As its first days would approach, he would recall how his mother would say that in the old shtetl even the fish in the lake would be visibly affected by the Elul atmosphere.

My father-in-law's death was not a tragedy in the usual sense of the word. He had lived a full and active life of more than eighty years, leaving behind a large family of children, grandchildren, and even great-grandchildren. But a death is always an unanticipated tragedy. Though he had been weak for the last few years, his sudden death was unexpected.

My children returned home from school just moments after I had learned the news. My older children were very saddened, flooded with memories of an active, kindly grandfather who had visited us many times in Toronto. My oldest son and daughter remembered how he had bought them their first real bicycles, a small red one and a larger pink one. Indelibly imprinted in their minds was his patience in sharing from his never-ending selection of stories of life in a different era, his interest in their studies, and, of course, his trail of wonderful presents.

My younger children, on the other hand, only had memories of our visits to my in-laws, seeing their *zeidy* for just a few moments in his weakened state before becoming too exhausted and needing to retire.

So I was a little taken aback by my youngest daughter's response to the news. A flood of genuine tears trickled down her soft cheeks. For a long time now she had been reciting a chapter of *Tehillim* (Psalms) on his behalf, and the finality of him being gone was especially traumatic for her young mind. It was hard for her to come to terms with never seeing her *zeidy* again. Even a weakened *zeidy*, whose memory was fading, was nevertheless a *zeidy*.

The next twenty-four hours passed in a blur of rushed activity — making arrangements to travel to Lakewood, New Jersey, where my husband had already arrived and where the funeral and shivah would take place.

Over the next couple of days, we would hear many stories about my husband's father from people whom he had helped in numerous ways, favors he had done and projects that he had been instrumental in launching. Many prominent rabbis, world-renowned *roshei yeshivah* (heads of learning academies), and communal leaders spoke about his lifelong devotion to building the Lakewood Yeshivah, where he served as its executive director until his retirement. They spoke, too, of his activism in starting Peylim, an organization whose mandate had been to ensure that every Jewish child in Israel had a Jewish education, and of his personal self-sacrifice any time any project — big or small — was needed for Jewish continuity. Many spoke of his idealism, his supreme honesty, or his strength of conviction and focus on spiritual goals, forgoing materialistic pursuits.

The stories, comments, and perspectives were encouraging for all of us to hear. I was especially gratified that my children learned of their *zeidy*'s monumental and lasting contributions. But one individual spoke of my father-in-law in a way that touched me more than any of the others.

As my husband stood up before the large crowd of prominent individuals, he began with great emotion, "I am trying to recall some of my earliest childhood memories of my father. But my mind is blank. I have none. I have no memories, because you, dear father, were never there."

He paused before the astonished crowd.

"You were never there, like so many other fathers, to take us on trips to the zoo or on family outings to the park. No, there weren't family games or short walks to get ice cream."

Once again he paused. He now had the audience's full attention.

"There were never these outings or trips because you were too busy. You left in the early hours of dawn before I awoke and often returned late at night, long after I had fallen asleep. You were always busy. Busy running to the *beit midrash* (study hall) to learn Torah... Busy running to help begin a new organization concerned about the plight of fellow Jews... Busy working nonstop to strengthen the values of Torah. When Shabbat finally came around, you were exhausted from your long, strenuous hours throughout the week.

"But though your physical presence might have been absent in those early years, you taught us, me and all your children, a powerful message. You taught us to value what was really important in life. You were willing to forego the normal pleasures of any father – what could be a greater pleasure for a father than taking his children to the zoo? – in order to help another Jew, in order to strengthen Torah in this country. And by doing so, you taught me so much more than any words could ever express.

"You taught me values. You taught me priorities. You taught me the need to reach out to other Jews and work tirelessly for a better tomorrow."

My husband concluded by saying, "Many people thought you were naturally an extrovert due to all of your projects, constantly conversing with so many people. But I, as your son, know that was not the case. You ignored your discomforts and pushed yourself to go out and do, very much against your nature, because you felt this was what was needed.

"And, dear father, I know that now, too, you will ignore your discomforts and push yourself. You will push yourself up on High to beg, plead, and demand from G-d to end our exile, our suffering and hardships."

My husband's words touched me deeply because of its important message. There are times when even in our absence or our silence — and, sometimes, *through* our absence and silence — we give over a message stronger than any words can possibly convey.

His message was one that my youngest daughter seemed to have intuitively picked up on. Even without the hours of contact and conversation with her grandfather that her older siblings had been privileged to experience, she had sensed, in our short, ten-minute visits, her *zeidy*'s message of love. Her *zeidy* was her *zeidy* who loved her — and it was this tragic loss that she cried genuine tears over.

My husband's message would bring comfort to us and to the whole family in the ensuing days, months, and years; the message and lesson of his father's life would endure even in his absence.

As the *yahrtzeit* candle burns perpetually on our kitchen counter, it isn't only his father's memory that we are keeping alive. More importantly, the continuing message of his life — the principles and values that he cherished and imparted to his children — continue to live on.

✎ *More than words can express, through our actions and values we send powerful, lasting messages to our children.*

The Girl with the Gold Watch

Toronto, 2005

I glance hurriedly at my wristwatch on this busy Friday after-noon, and I'm reminded of a story about a watch from another land and time.

My young daughter notices my far-off expression. I begin to describe to her a time when my own mother, Rebbetzin Batsheva Sudak-Schochet — her grandmother — was a youngster not much older than she.

"In that foreign land, observing Shabbat was not as simple as it is today, a matter of just adding an extra potato to a simmering pot of cholent," I explain while peeling potatoes. "For Savta, keeping Shabbat was a perilous practice — one that could cost dearly."

I begin to tell her of a time when the extra moment ticking on a gold watch provided the very gift of life...

Samarkand, 1943

The sounds of footsteps did not bode well for the young Sudak family, gathered around their Shabbat table. Adjacent to their home stood their underground soap factory. The factory was illegal in the Soviet Union, and its discovery could mean instant imprisonment, being sent to the front, or languishing in frigid Siberia for years.

But, as dangerous as it was, the factory also spelled the Sudaks' salvation, providing their sustenance while allowing them to avoid working on Shabbat. In those days of the Communist Party's all-out war on religion, observing Shabbat was not only an unheard of luxury that no employer would tolerate — it was a literal death sentence.

Rabbi Pinchas Sudak had taken all possible precautions to ensure that the factory's entrance was well hidden from any prying or meddling eyes, covered over by large planks of wood. But the approaching footsteps sounded like they knew where they were headed.

Someone had informed the authorities.

To the harsh sounds of wood being ripped apart, Pinchas and Batya made quick decisions.

"Pinchas, run away," Batya ordered. "If they arrest you, you will surely be sent to the front. I will remain with the children, vehemently denying that the factory belongs to me. Hopefully, the penalty will not be as grave for me, and they will have compassion for a lone mother with young children.

"Go now. Run, Pinchas!"

Pinchas gazed one last time at his beloved wife before hastily leaping off the high wall surrounding their home. With a prayer in his heart that he would again be reunited with his family, Pinchas fled, racing to avoid detection and capture, his heart beating wildly.

Batya was promptly led off to prison, leaving her oldest child, eleven-year-old Batsheva, to tend to her own horror and the fright of her two younger siblings, Nachman and Bracha.

But there wasn't time for the luxury of fright or tears. It was time for action.

Batsheva received a message via a family friend to immediately try to meet with her mother's interrogator, a cold-hearted female prosecutor who would determine the outcome of this case and who held the keys to her mother's freedom.

"Tell her that your mother does not own the factory," Batsheva was instructed. "Your father is in the army fighting valiantly for Mother Russia. The man who ran away was your mother's Polish friend who was helping the family make ends meet. He got the family into this illegal mess while your mother is innocent."

Because of the heavy Communist indoctrination of children in the school system, officials tended to believe young children who, often enough, would succumb to the brainwashing they underwent and convict their own parents for "crimes" committed against the State. Though only a girl, tall and mature Batsheva understood her grave responsibility and its sweeping implications. With immense faith and a heartfelt prayer on her lips, she squared her slight, young shoulders and confidently went to meet the prosecutor.

Batsheva convincingly told her tale and tearfully concluded, "Please, I miss her so much. I want my mother back!"

The prosecutor was touched by this attractive and personable young girl. "I'll see what I can do," she replied coolly.

The following day, Batsheva received a new message from her anxious father. "Go upstairs, into your mother's room, and open her drawer. You'll find an expensive gold watch. This time go to the prosecutor's home. Tell her you want to present her with this gift. Don't ask for anything in return, just explain to her that you want to see your mother."

Batsheva did as instructed. For the next few days, she kept a vigilant watch in front of the prison walls. She noticed her mother sitting outside on the cold ground, in a fenced-in area of the prison. She brought a coat for her to keep warm and delivered kosher food for her to eat.

Though it was comforting to see her mother, it was painful to see her behind bars in such woeful conditions. Those were difficult days for such a young girl, filled with intense anxiety about the future fate of her parents and family.

After two weeks, to Batsheva's surprised elation, her mother walked out of the prison door, a free woman. The prosecutor had closed the case, recording that the owner of the illegal factory was a Polish man who had fled upon its detection.

Pinchas remained in hiding. The plan was that Batya and her children would leave Samarkand as soon as possible, and the family would be reunited in far-off Tashkent.

Several weeks before their departure, on a Friday afternoon, Batsheva happened to meet up with the prosecutor on the street. The woman, who had taken a liking to Batsheva, amicably told her that she had "another case on this street."

Having grown up in the Soviet Union, Batsheva understood the veiled meaning of her words. A "case" could only bode ill for her people.

Immediately she informed her uncle, Rabbi Yisrael Leibov. He ran ahead to the home of Rabbi Binyamin Gorodetsky, who lived on that street, and warned him of the imminent danger. Rabbi Binyamin exited through his back door and raced to inform his brother, Rabbi Simcha, of the peril.

Rabbi Binyamin escaped and eventually left Russia to settle in Paris. Unfortunately, his brother didn't heed the warning and was imprisoned for ten long years.

Two weeks later, on a Friday morning before the Sudaks' departure from Samarkand, Batsheva was walking home from her grandmother's and once again met the prosecutor.

"I'll be making an arrest," she informed Batsheva matter-of-factly.

Again Batsheva ran to the home of her uncle, but this time he dismissed her warning, thinking that a young girl couldn't possibly be privy to such information.

Late that night, Batsheva's aunt was arrested and her passport confiscated.

Early the next morning, a pale and tense Rabbi Yisrael entered the Sudak home, asking Batsheva to bring some jewelry to the prosecutor. To the relief of the family, Batsheva was, once again, able to secure her aunt's release.

In the darkness of night, at the close of Shabbat, the Sudaks left Samarkand to make the long journey to Tashkent, over three hundred kilometers away. They hoped that the long arm of the Soviet secret police wouldn't follow them.

But that is a whole other story, not one to be told on a busy Friday afternoon...

Conscious of the approaching Shabbat, I pause to glance down at my wrist. A young girl... a gold watch...the holy day of rest...and the indomitable spirit and invincible faith of our people.

> ໑ *Within each of us lies untold power and courage. Tap into this hidden resource, and you will discover the strength to overcome any obstacles along your path.*

A Father's Blessings

Saying Goodbye

Parting has always been difficult for me. This is true for short-term partings and becomes exaggeratedly greater when a long separation is anticipated.

But never have I faced a parting as excruciatingly heart-wrenching as the one I recently experienced.

My family and I arrived in Cleveland on a Sunday afternoon. Early the following morning, my father, Rabbi Dovid Schochet, was scheduled for a serious operation which at his age and condition could be life-threatening.

For weeks, ever since the large growth was "accidentally" discovered on my father's kidney, the tension had built. It was a tumor of the sort known as the "silent killer," and my father was fortunate that it had been found through a series of unexpected tests. We all hoped that it wasn't too late for it to be contained.

In record time, due in no small part to my mother's vigilance and my sister and brother-in-law's perseverance, my father had been examined by several specialists in the field. Their prognosis was grim. They warned that speed was imperative to remove the cancerous growth before it spread any further. After that, there was nothing more they could do.

By divine providence, a series of events led my parents to a world-class specialist in Cleveland who hoped to successfully remove the growth and save the kidney. The doctor was a Canadian Jew with whom my father had exchanged some words of Torah during their initial meeting, and he felt confident that this doctor would be G-d's messenger to cure him.

Staying in a hotel adjacent to this famous Cleveland Clinic, our only comfort was in each other's presence.

It was late Sunday night, the night before the operation, and our collective anxiety engulfed each of us. My father emerged from his bedroom and joined my sister and me in the adjacent area. He sat down at the table, visibly nervous, and opened his book of *Tehillim*.

We watched him closely, not knowing what to say to encourage him. Several moments later, he concluded his reading and explained, "Tomorrow we will have to be in the hospital early, and I will be very rushed after the davening (prayers). I won't have time in the morning, so I wanted to recite the children's *Tehillim* tonight."

My father's custom, ever since I can remember, was to recite daily the chapters of *Tehillim* correlating with the age of each one of his many children and grandchildren.

It struck me that even at such a time he wouldn't miss praying on our behalf.

My father called my brother, who was staying a few blocks away. "Please meet us here at the hotel early tomorrow morning," he requested. "I want to make sure to *bentch* (bless) each of you before my surgery."

My father replaced the receiver, and I observed him intently while gulping down the large lump that was forming in my throat.

"Daddy," I said, "we don't want your blessing tomorrow. We want it after the surgery, for many years to come!"

My father smiled tolerantly at his youngest child and replied, "Yes, Chana, I definitely hope to bless all of you for many years to come. But tomorrow, too, is an auspicious opportunity, and one never knows…" His voice trailed off before he continued, "The final moments of life can be the most important ones. We are fortunate when we have a chance to prepare properly."

By now, it was past one o'clock in the morning. The alarm clock would buzz in four hours to awaken my father for the earliest minyan (prayer quorum). We would be leaving for the hospital shortly before seven o'clock.

I lay awake in bed, eyes open, scanning the strange room and picturing in my mind's eye my father blessing us, hoping that it would not be the final time. My mind restlessly grappled with the scene as my heart screamed, *How can I possibly say goodbye to someone who means so much to me? How can I convey to him through mere words my appreciation for his lifelong giving? And at such a juncture in his life, how can I finally give something back to him?*

The question twisted and turned in my anguished mind amid the doubt, hope, and fright wrestling there. Before long, morning mercifully dawned, providing an escape from the tormenting night.

My sisters, my mother, and I were waiting nervously by the time the men had returned from shul (synagogue). My father gathered his few personal belongings for the hospital in an overnight bag. He then stepped into the other room to call each of us, one by one, for a private, secluded moment of personal blessing.

Tears fell down my cheeks unabashedly as my oldest brother approached my father, whose face was white like the wall. Being the youngest of the family, I awaited my turn and in my thoughts considered how each of the twelve tribes must have felt, surrounding Yaakov (our forefather, Jacob) on his deathbed, receiving their last blessings and instructions as they bid him goodbye.

My father's beckoning to me broke my reverie, and I forced my feet, which felt like a pile of cement blocks, to move forward. He lifted his hands above my head and silently mouthed the traditional blessings. As he concluded, fresh tears stained my already wet cheeks, and he hugged me.

I gazed into his wise blue eyes, eyes that for so many years had looked at me with such teasing humor. I heard my voice say, "Daddy, thank you for being such a wonderful father all these years." And I had to suck in air since my chest felt like it would collapse under the crushing burden.

My father, who served as the beloved *rav* for more than forty-five years in the Toronto community, was more than a father. I forced myself to continue, "There hasn't been a day in my entire life that I haven't felt pride in being your daughter." I paused, then said, "But may G-d allow you to continue to be here for many years to come."

I noticed a tear escape my father's eyes. He nodded wordlessly as he hugged his youngest child once again, this time a touch tighter.

Moments later we all left the hotel together to walk the five-minute trek to the hospital surgery room.

The Wait

I sat in one of the lounges of the Cleveland Clinic surrounded by my mother, my siblings, and their spouses. Comfortable couches were arranged into discussion centers throughout this large lobby area. But instead of lively, animated chatter, the room was filled with a subdued undercurrent of talk, attesting to the tension filling this room, where families awaited news about the surgery of their beloved.

Off to the side of these areas, a large station marked "P20" stood. Equipped with computers, a paging system, phones, and other up-to-date technology, official-looking nurses busily attended to their work behind this counter with grim expressions on their faces. Families would descend on this station to request an update of the progress of the surgery. The nurses used pagers, handed to each family, to summon them from all parts of the large hospital.

It had already been several weeks since the initial news of the tumor found in my father's kidney. By now, we were well versed in the intricate aspects of his condition and well aware of the doctors' prognosis. Somehow, though, the news still hadn't sunk in and felt surreal.

About an hour ago, we tearfully left the bedside of my father as an intern wheeled him to the pre-operating room. I can't begin to imagine the emotions pulsing through him as he said the *vidui* (confession) prayer or as he bequeathed all his worldly goods as a gift of inheritance to my mother and informed us how his *sefarim* (books) should be divided should the worst occur. Nor can I fathom how he had the presence of mind to speak about the halachic (Jewish law) implications of burying his removed kidney or how he remembered to tell us to return a book he had borrowed from a local synagogue.

I marveled, too, at my mother's courage as she parted from my father, her husband of almost fifty years. She looked at him bravely and said, "You'll be all right. I know you will." She smiled encouragingly, but I was privy to the heart-wrenching turmoil and doubt she faced within.

The surgery was scheduled to last several hours. We sank comfortably into our couches, doing the only thing we could do: endlessly mouthing words of *Tehillim*, desperately entreating our Father in Heaven to grant my father many more years of earthly life. Hours passed with incessant words of prayers on our lips.

During this time, I glanced around the lobby and noticed many other families sitting and waiting. Some were whiling away their time with card games, while others were thumbing through popular magazines or newspapers. I felt immensely grateful to have the comforting gift of prayer so that I could utilize these strained hours constructively.

As the hours passed, I noticed many families leaving. Some gathered at the P20 station, exuberantly joyous. Others shuffled away, dejected and forlorn, their hearts shredded to pieces after learning a negative outcome.

I wouldn't realize it until later, but just such a scenario had haunted my father before his operation. When his own father was his age, my father's family sat in a similar hospital setting awaiting the news of my grandfather's surgery. The outcome then was not positive. His family was devastated when they were informed that the cancerous growth had spread. My grandfather, Rabbi Dov Yehuda Schochet, passed away shortly afterward.

At one point, I took a short walk around the lobby's corridors. I passed a large window facing one of the clinic's underground parking lots and observed the cars arriving and leaving. I thought how we, too, are parked in this world for a limited time. Silently I prayed that my father's time in this world had not yet expired. Unlike the cars, mere hunks of metal, I thought how each of us forms everlasting bonds of connection.

I remembered then that at this very hour scores of people, in yeshivah, synagogues, camps, and study groups around the world, were praying on my father's behalf. Countless individuals who had been touched by him had approached me, misty-eyed, on the streets or in the grocery store with their well wishes or whispered in my ear the good deed that they had taken upon themselves in his merit. I pictured all those prayers, all those positive acts, and all those chapters of *Tehillim* rising up, heavenward, providing an enormous spiritual shield. I felt somewhat comforted and strengthened.

A short while later the organizer of the Bikur Cholim (aid for the sick) organization of Cleveland came to greet us, laden with packages full of sandwiches and other refreshments.

Many come to Cleveland from around the world seeking the help of specialists from this reputable clinic. The Cleveland Jewish community responds to this with a remarkably organized and professional network of volunteers, providing all kinds of support, medical advice, meals, a place to stay, and anything else that a visitor might need. As this woman wished us well, we all felt enriched by more than the food that she had left with us.

My mother expressed it perfectly: "At a time like this, you really appreciate such unconditional outpourings of kindness."

The hours inched forward slowly. Then it was our turn at the P20 station. We learned that the operation had been successful. Thank G-d, the operation had concluded earlier than originally planned, the kidney was saved, the growth was removed, and it had not spread! We wouldn't know for certain for a few days, but from initial testing it appeared that the tumor was not cancerous — something that occurred in less than 5 percent of such cases.

Hearing such miraculous news, feeling overcome with relief and thanksgiving, my obvious reaction was to open my worn *Tehillim* once again. From the depths of my being, I expressed my gratitude to G-d.

Soon after, we rushed to the recovery room and pleaded with the nurse to allow us in to see my father. We stood at my father's bedside, our hearts bursting with joy and thankfulness as we watched my father open his eyes, smile weakly, and silently mouth *minchah*, the afternoon prayers.

I can't remember a sight as beautiful as seeing my mother gazing deeply into her husband's eyes. Words are not rich enough to describe the joy in her face as she stood almost wordlessly for close to an hour (until the nurse finally shooed us out), love and joy washing over her smiling features.

Two Farbrengens

I sat at my father's bedside on the night following his miraculously successful surgery. My brother and I would remain for the night, keeping a vigilant watch on my father.

I hadn't slept much the previous night, too full of anxiety before the operation, but now I was also too overwhelmed to even close my eyes. I sat still, intently watching my father's pale face, observing his calm breathing, grateful to have him with us.

"Close your eyes, Chana. Try to sleep," my father instructed, always considerate of another's well-being. But my eyes simply could not close. The tense events of the last several days coupled with the overwhelming relief of the miraculous outcome were too enormous for my mind to grapple with, and I needed the quiet reflection to digest it all.

I thought back to the last two weeks before the surgery. I remembered the tears each of us shed and the strength we mustered to take some action. I remembered hearing all about the doctors' visits and reports and finally the decision to come to this clinic.

I remembered, too, the *farbrengen* (chassidic gathering) we arranged at my home for my father, inviting the entire community. Many people attended, filling every chair and space in my home, toasting "*l'chaim*" (to health) to my father and singing heartfelt songs.

Chassidim say that the effect of a *farbrengen* is potent. We had hoped that it would be powerful now, too.

Years ago, my father's youngest sister had been helped through a *farbrengen*. My aunt, a young, rambunctious toddler, had fallen into my grandmother's boiling pot of laundry water. She was rushed to the hospital with her entire body scalded and with little hope for living.

The Lubavitcher Rebbe was immediately contacted, and he offered his blessing, some medical advice, and the instruction to my grandfather to hold a *farbrengen* celebrating her recovery. It must have been difficult for my grandparents to make a celebration when their daughter was lying in the hospital, close to the clutches of death. But soon after, my aunt miraculously and fully recovered.

Watching the many participants at my father's *farbrengen* and, later, watching my parents walking back home so regally, side by side,

I had hoped the same would be true with my father.

My mind skipped a few days later to the trip we had taken to the Ohel, the Lubavitcher Rebbe's grave site. My father, sister, brother-in-law, and I had flown into New York for the day, heading straight to the Rebbe's resting place to beseech him for a blessing on my father's behalf.

I stood in solemn prayer for a long time, expressing what I knew only the Rebbe could fathom. Standing opposite my father in the small area, I asked the Rebbe to intercede on behalf of this disciple of his, who had served as the Rebbe's emissary for so many years. I cried, too, for all the hardship and pain in the world, for all the wants and lacks, for all the needs, for all the negativity that we face.

Leaving the Ohel, my father turned to me and, paraphrasing the words of our Sages, blessed me, "May G-d fulfill all the desires of your heart."

I wanted to reply, "How could you possibly think of the desires of my heart at such a time?" but instead I quoted in return, " 'One who blesses shall himself be blessed.' "

Landing in Toronto late that night, I felt lighter, as if a crushing burden had been lifted from my heart, replaced instead with optimistic faith. I drove my father to his home, sixteen hours after having picked him up from there, and accompanied him to the door.

"Now that we've done what we can, all will be well," I stated emphatically.

"Yes, Chana. G-d willing, all will be well." And he hugged me.

And then my thoughts wandered to last Shabbat, only two days ago, but seeming like a world apart.

My children are accustomed to hear my husband relate stories about tzaddikim (righteous individuals) at our Shabbat table and eagerly await this part of our meal. This week my husband opened a newly published book and began to translate one of its stories.

To my astonishment, the story he had randomly chosen was about an individual who had a growth in his kidney. The man sought the opinion of several doctors, all of whom provided grim forecasts, before consulting with the Rebbe. Several weeks later, with the Rebbe's blessing and to the doctors' complete befuddlement, the growth had entirely vanished. Hearing the story, I felt the Rebbe's warm embrace, encouraging us that all would be fine.

I smiled contentedly at my father in his hospital bed now, these scenes playing out before my eyes, grateful for the miraculous results. Eventually I dozed into a restless slumber, sitting upright in a hospital chair, pillow propped up behind my head.

I awoke suddenly. My father was calling to my brother, "Yossi, Yossi."

"What is it, Daddy? Are you in pain?" I was quickly on my feet, at his side.

"It's morning, so it is time for davening. Yossi, you need to go to the minyan," my father, who was always diligent in this matter, urged my brother.

My brother opened his groggy eyes and turned on the main light switch. We both dissolved into laughter, seeing that the clock read 5:15 a.m.

We looked at each other knowingly. It was wonderful to have our father back.

> ❧ *When facing a potential loss, we come to fully realize how the contributions of our parents or mentors have made us into who we have become. It is up to us to pass on this legacy to our children and students.*

Hospitality, 1939

The year was 1939. The Second World War had been raging for some months. The Jews in the Soviet Union, like the Jews the world over, were not yet aware of the horrendous events transpiring across the border in Poland, where the wholesale slaughter and genocide of their brethren by the barbaric Nazi murderers was already under way.

Pinchas Sudak, who was living in Russia, had no idea that within a few short years entire communities would be wiped out. But he suspected that something was amiss.

There were ominous signs emerging from Poland as more and more Polish Jews began fleeing the country, even preferring to come to the dreaded Soviet Union than to remain in their homeland. Men, women, and children were seeking refuge, hoping merely for the gift of life. Respected communal leaders, wealthy philanthropists, and ordinary people from all walks of life had become wanderers overnight, seeking asylum and a roof over their heads and some nourishment for their empty stomachs.

These Polish Jewish refugees would arrive at the train station in Russia with nothing left of their worldly possessions except for the small suitcases clutched in their arms. They arrived in this hostile land, where the language and customs were strange to them, with not a friend in the world and knowing no one to whom they could turn.

The Soviet government reacted to their guests with typical suspicion and cruelty. Under the ruse of claiming them possible "enemies of the state," the government forbade any contact with these foreigners. The refugees would sleep in the open stations, exposed to the elements, awaiting deportation to frigid Siberia. Any Russian citizen communicating with these "foreign spies" would be threatened and penalized with imprisonment.

In that climate of desperation, Pinchas and Batya Sudak opened up their home. To them, it was unthinkable to desert one's brethren in such a time of need, and they actively and resolutely sought out these refugees, despite the great personal danger.

Several times a week Pinchas traveled to the train station along with his eldest daughter, Batsheva. He wrote out a note in Yiddish, briefly stating, "If you want a warm meal, come to..." with the exact address and directions to his home.

"Batsheva, approach the Polish children as if you are looking at their strange clothing," Pinchas instructed his daughter.

The Polish refugees wore different clothing and tucked their pants into their socks, a custom considered bizarre in Russia. It wouldn't arouse suspicion if a young child approached these children out of curiosity.

"Hand them this note, and we will have the mitzvah of helping our fellow Jews."

Though only seven years old, Batsheva understood the implications of her actions. Deftly and courageously, she would slip the note to the youngsters, acting as a curious child who had mischievously wandered away from her father.

The Polish Jews were immensely grateful for this extended lifeline. One by one, they would slip away and come to the Sudak home to be greeted warmheartedly with a nourishing meal and a place to rest.

On some Friday nights, so many refugees arrived at the Sudak home that a few had to sleep on the floor for lack of any other space. Occasionally, if the police would make a routine check, Pinchas warned his guests to exit rapidly through the back doors or windows as he went to open up the front door, feigning innocence.

Pinchas understood the risk to his family's lives and security. But there was no question in his or his wife Batya's mind that this was their duty.

One time, among the group of Polish Jews that found their way to the Sudak home, there was one particular individual who stood out from the rest. He wore a beautiful and expensive fur-lined coat, and, unlike so many of the downtrodden refugees, he had an aura of confidence about him and carried himself like a distinguished person.

Pinchas was pleased to host him during their Friday night meal and spent time conversing with him. But he noticed that Batya seemed uncomfortable with him. She hastily put away their expensive dishes and silverware, which usually graced the Sudak Shabbat table.

Toward the end of the meal, the individual asked to remain in the Sudak home for the night. Seeing his wife's discomfort, Pinchas slipped into the kitchen for a private consultation with her. He was certain that, as always, Batya would be happy to open their home to this respected individual.

"Absolutely not," was Batya's forceful response. "Not him! He may not sleep in our home."

Pinchas was astounded by this reaction, so contrary to his wife's usual generous spirit. He tried to dissuade her at first, but, seeing her strong stance, regretfully explained to his guest that since his wife was not feeling well, it would not be possible for him to stay with them overnight.

At the end of the meal, Pinchas accompanied his guest to the door. He helped him with his coat and walked him out toward the street.

When Pinchas returned, his face was ashen. "How did you know?" he asked Batya incredulously.

"What happened?" Batya responded.

"As I lifted our guest's coat, I felt something hard inside. I could discern the shape of three large knives. The man was an imposter! A robber! I pretended that I hadn't noticed his weapons and respectfully walked him out toward the street. Had we let him stay overnight, he certainly would have killed us all and robbed our home!"

The words tumbled from Pinchas's mouth. He paused for a moment, thinking about the disastrous implications. "But how were you able to tell?"

"I just sensed something about him I didn't like," Batya answered.

The merit of the Sudaks' *hachnasat orchim* (hospitality) prevented them from coming to harm. This unfortunate scare, however, did not prevent the Sudaks from continuing to host their brethren and to assist them even after they left their home.

Pinchas made inquiries about the fate of several Polish Jews whom he had hosted and learned that they had been sent to Siberia. He sent food packages regularly to as many families as possible. He knew how invaluable these packages would be for them. For his own and his family's safety, he did not write from whom these packages originated nor his return address.

One time Pinchas did receive a letter back from a Polish Jew who realized that he was the benefactor. He thanked Pinchas for his benevolence and explained to him how "we shared your generous food with another member of our group who was slowly starving to death. This individual reminded us that in two weeks is the nineteenth day of Kislev." These veiled words were a reference to the chassidic holiday of Yud Tet Kislev, a day commemorating the first Chabad Rebbe's liberation from Soviet prison.

Though Pinchas never found out the man's identity, he was gratified to learn that he had saved the life of a fellow Chabad chassid.

Some nameless individual who was imprisoned due to his "anti-Communist" work — that is, spreading *Yiddishkeit* and teaching Torah to young children — was saved due to his efforts.

On another occasion, the Sudaks hosted an individual who, despite his modest demeanor, had a regal bearing, refined features, and was well versed in all areas of Torah. Immediately Pinchas sensed that this was a special person and invited him to remain in his home for as long as he needed. The man, Hersh Melech, hesitated, knowing that he had no money to pay for this generosity.

Pinchas convinced him to stay by suggesting that Hersh Melech tutor his young son, Nachman, in exchange for the hospitality. Hersh Melech agreed and remained for almost two years in the Sudak home.

Several years later, after the Sudak family had escaped from Russia and were settled in Israel, a large entourage of chassidim drove up to their home. The Rebbe of this group, dressed in regal clothing, knocked on the Sudaks' door and greeted the family warmly.

He explained to Pinchas that he had to come in person to visit them and to thank them for the kindness they had extended to him when he had arrived, a penniless refugee, in the Soviet Union back in 1939.

Pinchas welcomed him in and, turning to Batsheva, asked if she recognized the man.

How could she not? It was none other than the unassuming "Hersh Melech."

⤷ *G-d ensures us safety and success when we endure sacrifices in following His will.*

Full Circle:
My Zeidy's Sefer Torah

S hortly after the Second World War, my maternal *zeidy*, Rabbi Pinchas Sudak, and his family escaped from Communist Russia. Along their dangerous trek, Zeidy Pinchas purchased a *sefer Torah* (Torah scroll). This is the story of that very special *sefer Torah*.

Unlike most Jews living under the Communist Soviet regime, Zeidy Pinchas did not lack for anything. He had an underground knitting factory and was a relatively wealthy man. He also managed to maintain an observant Jewish lifestyle for himself and his family. When he escaped from Russia in the summer of 1946, at the age of thirty-eight, it was not because of any material or even spiritual need, nor did he do it for the spiritual future of his children.

Zeidy Pinchas risked being shot at the border for trying to escape for the sake of his grandchildren.

My mother, Batsheva — the oldest of Zeidy Pinchas's three children — grew up in a home where commitment to Judaism was a way of life. As a young girl, she would ride alone on a donkey for several miles through the desert to bring home the wheat that would later be grinded and prepared under exacting supervision for the Pesach (Passover) matzah. That was her task because, as a child, she was not as subject to questioning by the authorities.

It wasn't unusual in my mother's home for music books to be swiftly spread over the piano as soon as a stranger entered their home, hiding the religious books nesting beneath. In this way, my mother was able to pursue her Jewish studies with her "piano teacher."

Zeidy Pinchas recognized that his children, raised to fight for the preservation of their faith, would gain inordinate strength to persevere in following the path of their tradition — no matter what the circumstances.

"I am not leaving Russia for my own children," he said. "They will always know that they are Jews and will remain loyal to their faith. But what will become of my children's children? That I do not know. It is for them that I must escape the clutches of this regime."

Fortunate to have crossed the Russian border alive, the Sudak family found themselves in Cracow with a group of forty-six other chassidim escaping the Stalinist dictatorship, their final destination unknown.

There, in Cracow, Zeidy Pinchas met a Polish Jew who was offering a Torah scroll for sale, and he resolved immediately to purchase the Torah. He had a heavy wooden box fashioned to carry and protect it.

"Wherever this journey may lead us," said Zeidy Pinchas, "how can so large a group of Jews travel without a *sefer Torah* in their midst?"

It was time for the group to move onward. They walked through Steczen to cross the Czechoslovakian border on their way to Prague. They left late at night. Each could carry only his most basic necessities; all other worldly possessions were abandoned. Zeidy Pinchas had diamonds sewn into the soles of his family's shoes.

In the blackness of the night, Zeidy Pinchas and Bubby Batya and their three children, each grasping a coarse rope to keep them together, trekked silently through a dense forest. Zeidy Pinchas clutched his beloved *sefer Torah* as he marched behind Bubby Batya, who carried their youngest child, Bracha. As time progressed, Bubby Batya grew weary and motioned to her husband that she could no longer carry Bracha.

With tears in his eyes, Zeidy Pinchas took his *sefer Torah* out of its wooden case and silently mouthed an apology. "My priceless Torah, you know that it is for you that I have left Russia. I would not have left to an unknown future for myself, nor for my children. I am fleeing to ensure that my children's children will know you and live with you. Forgive me, dear Torah, for betraying you now. It is either you or my child. I part with you now, so that my children and children's children should live a life of which you are a real and meaningful part."

He embraced the Torah for the last time and gently laid it, in its case, under a tree. Then he lifted his young child in his arms and journeyed forward.

Eventually, Zeidy Pinchas and his family reached the free shores of Israel. His children, Batsheva, Nachman, and Bracha, grew up to become rabbis or *rebbetzin*s, serving their respective communities and promulgating faith in Torah.

❧ ❧

A few years ago, my mother, Rebbetzin Batsheva Schochet, was visiting in California, and she was invited to the home of Mrs. Faigy Estulin, a friend of my sister's. Faigy was describing her own father's exodus from Russia — several weeks after my grandparents' escape — and attributed his longevity and robust health to an incident that happened more than fifty years ago.

He and his wife were escaping Russia on a dark night. Along the way, their five-year-old daughter wandered away from them and was momentarily lost. Frantically, the parents searched for her, crawling on their hands and knees through the forest.

Suddenly Rabbi Gurevitch felt something hard. Upon further investigation, he found a wooden box and opened it. Inside was a *sefer Torah*.

Next to the wooden box sat his young child.

Kissing both passionately, he took the Torah from its box, unraveled it, and wrapped it around his body, tying it with his *gartel* (prayer belt). Eventually, that Torah scroll made its way to its current home, in a synagogue in New York City.

Mrs. Estulin ended by crediting her father's long and healthy life to the merit of this significant act.

Upon concluding her story, she looked up at my mother and couldn't fathom why my mother's face had gone completely ashen and tears were streaming from her eyes.

The legacy of Zeidy's precious *sefer Torah* had come full circle.

Having heard this story, a cousin of mine asked me jokingly, "Great story. But where are the diamonds that were in our parents' shoes?"

Smiling, I answered, "We, Zeidy's grandchildren and great-grandchildren, are those diamonds. And the dividends are in our good deeds."

> *Enduring sacrifices for your beliefs proves their value. Such teachings provide your children with the strength, identity, and direction to face their own hardships.*

These journal questions reflect values from the stories you just read. Record your answers for a greater awareness of your spiritual perspective on life.

On Identity
JOURNAL

1. Identify three significant mentors in your life.

2. How have you grown from their examples?

3. List the qualities you admire about your mentors.

4. Which of these qualities would you like to emulate? What practical steps are you taking to access those qualities?

5. Identify something positive that your parent or grandparent did. What have you learned from it?

6. What silent messages are you sending to your family and friends about your priorities or values in life?

On Potential

Living with Inspiration

This past Monday morning I awoke, like every day, except that this morning I was uninspired.

I worked my way through my regular schedule, which I often find a surprising challenge, with bored disinterest. It all seemed far too tedious, even irrelevant.

I searched for the meaning and inspiration that I usually associate with the multifaceted obligations in my life, but I found none. It had been replaced with a sea of monotony and purposelessness, a rush of activity with little meaning or direction.

The rush hour of getting the kids clothed, breakfasted, and carrying their brown-bagged lunches as they scurried out the front door to their honking car pools was over. I now found a moment to drink in the sinking blandness in my mind and savor its dullness over my cup of steaming coffee. Even its freshly percolated aroma, usually so rich, this morning smelled and tasted unstriking.

Nor did the day progress any better.

I tried to pray passionately, to ask You for guidance and direction to help me find the meaning that I lacked. I even attempted to complain to You angrily about all the suffering and hardship in Your world that the newspapers bombard us with daily. I tried to muster some emotion, if not gratitude, at least anger, pain, or frustration. Something. Anything. But nothing came. Instead, the words came out automatically, in a monotone, as tasteless as my morning coffee had been.

At the office I went through the regular motions, taking care of the paperwork, updating the data on the computer, returning phone calls, organizing upcoming adult educational programs, and scheduling my calendar. But it was all without emotion, without passion. I whiled away the hours with a growing restlessness, looking forward to being back at home.

I drove the short distance from my office to home. Trying to drown the thoughts in my mind, I played the Jewish music cassette loudly. It sang Your praise, the sweetness of Your ways, Your merits and our gratitude to You. But as loud as it played, my mind screamed its dissent even louder. Why? Why were life's challenges so difficult? Why was there so much pain? What was the purpose of it all? Are You really enjoying watching us constantly repeat our blunders only to face them yet again? Isn't there a better way?

I knew that my soul was sad that Monday. I knew that she was hurting. Yet I also knew that I couldn't reach her, caress her, or provide her with the balm of spiritual nourishment that she so desperately craved.

My soul was imprisoned behind a thick, coarse wall of absolute and complete, dispassionate, and uninspiring apathy.

For a few moments that sunny afternoon, I thought that I had almost grabbed hold of her. In a few quiet moments, as my youngest child sat on my lap and I read to him his favorite tales, I smelled sweetness in the air. Sitting side by side with him on the bare wood floor as we built an elaborate structure of the Beit HaMikdash (Holy Temple) with his colorful wooden blocks, I thought that I had tasted some meaning.

To my disappointment, it was elusive and disappeared again in the ensuing busy moments as the regular routine resumed.

Nor did my mood improve when I remembered that today was Monday and I was slated to deliver my weekly Monday night Torah class to the regular, full-capacity crowd. The class had grown, and some fifty or sixty women attended. They looked to this class for their weekly inspiration, their connection to You and to spirituality. How, I wondered, would I bring them inspiration when I couldn't find any myself?

Evening rolled around, and I was physically drained, but even more emotionally and spiritually exhausted. All I wanted was to curl up in my bed and allow sleep to overtake me, to stop my mind's incessant thoughts and hope to awaken to a more rewarding tomorrow.

Instead, dutifully, I put on a fresh gloss of lipstick and grabbed a smartly matching blazer as I grudgingly headed out the door.

As I entered the large room of the synagogue, a feeling of dread washed over me. Of course, a welcoming smile was plastered over my face, but within was turmoil.

To my surprise, the class progressed well. We delved into the sources and applied its lessons to our lives. The questions from the audience were interesting. Somehow, my mouth and tongue worked in partnership and found the right words and resources, and the participants left, to my relief, enlightened and inspired.

As I once again opened the front door of my home, I wondered at the change in my mood. What had happened? What had "reconnected" me? At what moment did inspiration replace apathetic doom and gloom?

I knew it had not been the words that I had said, for there was nothing novel about them. I was certain, too, that it was not the material covered, as that, too, was very familiar to me. And though the participants' questions were challenging and their comments engaging, they did not reveal any new revelation or perspective.

So what was it that during the day I was unable to reach, with my prayers, Torah learning, or my daily rituals and routines, that this room, surrounded by these women, had unlocked?

Pondering these thoughts, I realized that though there was nothing novel in what I had said, I was forced, due to the circumstances, to say it passionately. Surrounded by those women looking to me for inspiration, I was forced to perform a drama, to act out an inspiration, to find a meaning and a purpose that I hadn't perceived.

And as I allowed myself to act out this inspiration, I surprised myself by actually feeling it. The act became experienced; the passion became real. And, in the process, the connection became established.

I learned something essential about inspiration on that bland and uninspirational Monday.

Sit back and wait for the inspiration to surface, as one awaits the sun to peak through the dense fog on a cloudy day, and you won't find it. Allow yourself to chase it, to act it and to experience it, and it will emerge. Suddenly the walls of apathy will crumble as you come into contact with the true inner depths of yourself.

Listen intently to the voice that emerges. You may even hear your own soul speaking.

ॐ Tap into your inner strength and calling by finding something that you can act passionately for.

In the Fitting Room of the Soul

Women love shopping.

Just ask their husbands. They'll tell you.

A woman may have had a stressful day or a doom-and-gloom outlook on life. But a short escape to the nearest mall to buy herself a new sweater, a scarf, or any other small accessory, and suddenly life looks a little brighter.

It's a pretty benign habit — if you're careful not to overtax your credit card.

So the other day, with fifteen minutes to spare and desperately in need of a break, I headed off to my favorite department store. Within moments I had skimmed the aisles, spotted my purchase, tried it on, and was standing in line waiting my turn at the checkout counter.

The jacket was the right size, a great fit, just my color (a perfect blend of browns and beige), had a designer label, and was reduced to a price I just couldn't resist. Add to that the saleslady's encouraging remarks ("It was made for you") and the nods of approval from fellow shoppers in adjacent changing rooms, and it seemed like a sure win.

Of course, in the back of my mind I knew that though the jacket fit in size, it didn't really fit in style. To be honest, it was kind of bulky and uncomfortable for indoor wear. I think I even had a similar one sitting in the back of my closet. But the color was exactly what I was looking for, and didn't they all acknowledge how well it suited me?

Later I recalled that a person's thoughts, speech, and actions are termed the "garments of the soul." Just as we express who we are through the clothes we choose to wear, so does the soul express its longings and wants, capabilities and talents — its unique self — by "clothing" itself in thoughts, spoken words, and actions.

Sometimes we allow ourselves to choose clothes that fit our style. We act, think, and speak compatibly with the true goals of our lives. We carefully select those "garments" that should be incorporated into our wardrobes and those that should be bypassed.

At other times, though, external factors sidetrack us. It may be social pressures, attractive colors, or an external fit. Whatever the case, we ignore the most important factor: is this really expressing the me that I feel comfortable with? Do they feel right and comfortable with the person I want to be?

Comes a time when we may need to reassess our life's purchases, big or small. Then you may find yourself standing exactly where I was the next time I had fifteen minutes to spare.

This time I was at a different counter. It had a sign above it reading "Customer Service."

After all, I'll only shop in stores where returns are gladly accepted.

➣ *Ask yourself honestly whether the life choices you are making are in tune with your inner goals.*

The Day I Became an Artist

Me an artist? Not quite.

The most I'll ever venture — after extensive pleading from my children — is a rather crude stick figure or a makeshift bird or flower, drawn exactly as I drew it when I was ten.

Fortunately, my husband is artistic, and several of my children inherited his artistic flair. Any school assignment or project that my younger children bring home requiring the slightest creative dexterity gets immediately delegated to his far more capable hands. Try as I might, my sketches never quite match up, so why even bother when surrounded with such talent?

So it was with some bemusement that I accepted an invitation from Marta to spend an afternoon in her home viewing her artwork.

Marta is a friend of mine who for several years, off and on, has attended my Torah classes. She is also an accomplished artist whose works hang in several major galleries. I wondered, at first, how I would relate to Marta's talent. But after continued requests from Marta, our schedules finally coincided, and we made a date to get together at Marta's home.

Marta enthusiastically invited me in to the sound of soft music playing in the background. Her home was designed as an open, airy space with light wood floors and soft fluid colors throughout. She began showing me around, and I got the distinct impression that Marta's home was more than a home, but a self-styled gallery of her novel exhibits.

Every wall in Marta's home was graced with a portrait, abstract illustration, sculpture, or drawing. Each framed work had a poetic title, and Marta elaborated on its meaning as we walked around the rooms. She explained how each piece tangibly portrayed a different time period in her life, an experience or a passage that she had gained from.

Marta used many mediums for her self-expression. There was a piece titled *A Voyage of Expression* in which Marta had created a square, metallic shape with steps that could be turned in many directions. The steps portrayed one's growth through life's circumstances. Depending on how the medium was turned, the steps could be heading upward or downward. Marta clarified how we can utilize the transitions of our passages to soar to great heights or to fall to abysmal depths, depending on our perspectives and choices.

Bonds of Time was another piece, sculpted in the form of a feminine head and bound with a thick winding cord. It represented the umbilical cord and the strong connection tying a mother together with her children at all periods of their lives.

There were many more of these creations, carved from an assortment of metals. But all the creations had a message and captured a realization that Marta had uncovered through her life's experiences.

Afterward, Marta explained why she had wanted me to view her art. "I've been reading your books, Chana, and I've been attending your classes. I see you are doing in your writing and teaching what I do through my art."

I stared at her uncomprehendingly as she continued, "You've experienced a realization, a higher knowledge that you wish to communicate to others. Through your personal expression, your mediums of speech and writing, you are sharing with others your perceptions and deeper understandings. Through your convictions, you are changing the mediums of our world into a better place."

Marta taught me a lot about how to view art that afternoon.

I had always viewed art as simply the ability to accurately copy or duplicate a (usually) pretty form onto a paper or canvas. Chassidic philosophy explains, however, that art is really the artist's ability to step away from the externalities of a thing and, disregarding its outer form, gaze into its innerness, perceive its essence. In this way, the artist sees new meaning, and the object is revealed as it has never before been seen, causing the one who looks at it to perceive it in another, truer light.

Marta tangibly illustrated to me that afternoon how to view artistic expression. She especially showed me that, regardless of our artistic dexterity, we are all artists.

Our world is our empty canvas. Our individualistic personalities are our brushes. And our special talents are our paints.

Throughout our lives, each of us is completing a unique portrait that we are bequeathing to our surroundings.

∾ *Every act and deed that we perform forms our individual, one-of-a-kind contribution to our world.*

Carrying His Own Keys

"Rabbi Schochet, I must speak with you."

The man, wearing blue jeans and a faded gray T-shirt, unexpectedly stomped into my father's office just as he was leaving for a meeting.

It was the first time that my father had seen this man, and he came without a prior appointment. He looked agitated and rushed, his brows creased in tension. He was holding a green apple in one hand and a magazine in the other. He sat himself down on the nearest chair and, without giving my father a chance to greet him, spoke again.

"Rabbi, I want proof that G-d exists," he demanded, to my father's astonishment.

"Let me explain. I have been dating a non-Jewish woman for a while. I love her deeply, and we are perfect for each other. The only problem is my family. They keep insisting to me that G-d frowns at this relationship. I've decided to ignore their repeated pleas, and I plan to move on with my life and marry her." He paused to catch his breath.

"This morning, though, I had a gnawing doubt and decided to speak with a rabbi first. If you can prove to me that G-d exists, without a shadow of a doubt, I will not marry her. If not," his voice sounded hard and almost threatening, "I will proceed with the marriage plans."

That was a tall order for anyone and in particular with a scheduled meeting pressing and a man who looked too distressed to calmly discuss things thoroughly.

"And if I do prove this to you, you will no longer have anything to do with this woman?" my father questioned firmly.

"Yes, I promise that I will drop her," the man answered emphatically.

"Look at what you are holding," my father said. "The apple in your hand reveals the existence of G-d."

Ignoring the man's puzzled expression, my father took out a pocketknife from his drawer and reached across his desk for the green apple. He sliced it lengthwise in half, juice dripping over the papers on his desk. "Do you see the five stars and ten dots shaped on the inside of the apple? Every single apple was fashioned in this way. Each one has this element of five and ten. Do you know why? Every apple reveals to us and reminds us of the saying of our Sages, 'With Y-ah G-d created the world.' " (Y-ah is one of G-d's Names, which contains a *yud* and a *hei, yud* signifying the tenth letter of the Hebrew alphabet and *hei*, the fifth letter.)

The man had been listening intently. He smiled momentarily, and the tension on his face decreased somewhat. "That is very interesting, Rabbi. Yes, that is an interesting proof."

He paused for a moment, in quiet reflection, but then the crease of tension returned to his features. "Scientifically it is definitely a curious phenomenon. And how coincidental that I was carrying just such a fruit. But, nevertheless, I am not entirely convinced that this is conclusive proof for the existence of G-d."

He was considering making a monumental change in his life and was searching for something stronger.

"Let me see the other thing you are holding — your magazine. It, too, proves G-d's existence."

My father was referring to the *Reader's Digest* in the man's other hand. My father opened it up arbitrarily, and his face paled as he quietly scanned the contents of the page.

The words he read aloud to the man sitting opposite him searching for G-d's existence and for newfound faith were the words that Jews have said daily for thousands of years, in its original Hebrew, transliterated into English.

In a clear and loud voice, from the pages of the *Reader's Digest*, my father read, "*Shema Yisrael Ad-nai Elokeinu Ad-nai echad* – Listen, dear Jews, G-d is our G-d, G-d is one."

My father had "coincidentally" opened up to an essay describing different children's prayers throughout the world written by a Jewish woman. On this particular page in the *Digest*, she was describing a childhood memory, when her aged grandmother taught her the Shema prayer, prayed by Jews throughout the millennia declaring their faith in the Oneness of G-d. She had written the prayers in English transliteration based on the original Hebrew that her grandmother had painstakingly taught her.

The man was dumbstruck, and with a tear rolling down his cheek he whispered, "Yes, Rabbi Schochet, if G-d has made this encounter happen this morning, I, too, now have conclusive proof that there is a G-d."

❧ ❧

When my father recounted this story, the cynical part of my personality asserted itself. I asked him how he was able to perform such "miraculous tricks" and what made him even think of attempting it?

"What if it wouldn't have worked, and you wouldn't have opened up to that page, what then? I mean, Daddy, *Reader's Digest* isn't exactly the first place that I would look to conclusively prove G-d's existence. Weren't you taking a tremendous risk?"

"Chana," he responded, "look at the circumstances. By divine providence the man found his way into my office. I had never met him before, and had he arrived even a moment later, I would no longer have been there.

"So I thought to myself, *There is a plan and a role that G-d is orchestrating here.* Whenever an individual has a problem, question, or issue, the solution has already been determined and is right there before him. He merely needs to open up his understanding to discover it.

"Like that man, we, too, carry the very solution that we seek. It is within our grasp; in fact, we are holding it right in our own hands.

"Furthermore, our Sages teach, '*Shlucho shel adam kemoso —* Someone's messenger has the power of the initial sender.' We are simply pawns and players enacting G-d's Grand Plan. It is not our own powers or abilities that cause our success or achievements, but that of the One who sends us.

"We must never shy away from playing our part, though. Never fear, my child, to use your abilities to their utmost. Never worry about taking the plunge in fear of the outcome. Because, in truth, you are not falling back on your own strengths or resources; you are being granted infinite powers, far beyond your own."

My father never did make his meeting that afternoon, but a lost soul started on his journey back to his people.

༄ *Realize that you carry the keys to unlock your own doors of potential. Understanding this provides you with an essential awareness and confidence about your capabilities.*

Up, Up, and Away

Spring was in the air. It was one of the very first warm days after an endlessly bleak winter season. Naturally my children and I enthusiastically welcomed the change by basking outdoors in the brilliant sunshine.

Settling into a lawn chair strategically placed to make the most of the sun's beaming rays, I gazed at my children playing alongside the sidewalk. Shira and Yisroel had begun a game of catch with Shira's new Superball.

The small red-and-blue-checkered ball was bouncy and, once released from Shira's grip, soared high into the deep azure sky. Higher and higher it climbed as Yisroel opened his small arms wide in anticipation. But, freed from its jail of gravity, the Superball took on a life of its own as it danced and glided right past his outstretched hands.

The two children scampered along the walkway to unearth the missing ball's whereabouts. Their search proved fruitless, and a moment later the two were at my side, yanking at my arm.

"We can't find my ball, Mommy," Shira said dejectedly.

"Yes," four-year-old Yisroel confirmed. "Shira threw it to me, and it went up, up, up, so high." He demonstrated by stretching his arms up as far as he could. "But then the ball got lost somewhere."

"Can you please help us find it?" Shira entreated, tugging at me more vigorously.

Attempting to stall them and absorb the sun's radiant rays for another moment, I jokingly offered, "Maybe the ball is still stuck somewhere up, up, up, high in the sky."

Shira giggled at the thought of a ball suspended in midair, but Yisroel took my suggestion seriously and proceeded to refute my stance.

"No, no," he explained patiently, shaking his head. "The ball *never* just stays still. If it's not going higher, it must be falling down."

My son's words struck a chord as I thought how we, too, are like a thrown ball, bursting with unbridled energy, talents, and vitality.

But with that potent energy comes choices. We can use our energy and potential to direct our lives upward — to become better people dedicated to higher ideals of honesty, ethics, and compassion. Or the same energy can lead us on a downward spiral leading to self-centered, corrupt, and fallen human beings.

One thing is for sure, though. The ball *never* remains stationary, suspended in midair. If you're not in the process of surging upward, you are sure to find yourself falling downward.

༷ *Don't content yourself with your present accomplishments. Strive to reach higher. The moment you cease climbing, you begin sliding.*

First Snow

I n the Canadian winter, it snows. And snows. And snows.

Yet no matter how much snow we get, for my children, the initial snowfall is always the most enthralling. Almost magical.

This morning was our first snowstorm of the season. We woke up engulfed in layers upon layers of white stuff. Snow covered the roads, it coated our porch, and it blanketed our front steps. It left a thick film of fluffy whiteness over the street lamps, the rooftops of neighboring houses, and the naked trees.

My children, as if on cue, woke up eagerly to greet this new winter wonderland. Gazing out our front window, they were impatient to get outside.

"It's really too cold out there," I responded to their repeated pleas. "Maybe later."

"We'll bundle up," they stubbornly insisted. And even the youngest, who usually requires some assistance, dressed himself instantly, adorned in a scarf, hat, gloves, and boots according to my exact specifications.

I glanced at the snow, and I wanted to crawl back under my

warm covers. My children saw it and were enchanted by its allure.

To me, the snow was cold and frigid. To them, it was exhilarating.

To me, it signaled winter's arrival and, of necessity, would have to be dealt with. To them, it was a new and invigorating environment filled with vast potential for fun and vivacity.

To me, the snow was burdensome, cumbersome. To them, it was something to experience, to feel, touch, handle, and manipulate.

To me, it implied the chores of shoveling, the urgency of finding the right partner for each boot and glove. To them, it meant the opportunity to create new forms, to mold new shapes. It presented a whole world of innovation.

I tried hard to remember back to the time when I, too, looked at snow with the ardent anticipation that my children did. I tried to rejuvenate my own perspective by reflecting on their attitude to snow and, by extension, to life in general.

I thought of how our soul wakes up every morning, at the crack of dawn, refreshed and enthusiastic to begin its new day. It, like my children, passionately waits to get its hands involved with the work of our world. Zealously it anticipates getting busy molding creation, touching and experiencing the many facets and aspects of our world to make it a better place.

It is ablaze with impatience to pray fervently, to study Torah intensely, to extend itself in doing a favor or sharing a smile of encouragement.

Our experienced and jaded self, though, complains to the soul: It's too cold; it's too cumbersome. Maybe we'll pray or study or do an act of kindness later. We'd rather get back under our covers.

Gradually, we deal with what needs to be taken care of, but out of necessity. Do we merely shovel it away? Have we forgotten the magic, the childlike joy and excitement in the process?

After some time outdoors, my children came back inside. Seated around the kitchen table, they warmed their frozen fingers and defrosted their bright, red cheeks while nibbling on snacks and sipping hot chocolate. Each one enthusiastically described all the shapes and forms he or she had created.

We sat like that not more than fifteen minutes, resting and enjoying the warmth of each other's company, when, to my chagrin, my youngest child unexpectedly asked, "Can we go back outside again now?"

&c *Tap into your childlike energy, enthusiasm, and optimism by realizing your power to mold your surroundings into a better world.*

When the Shoe Fits

As youngsters, my best friend and I used to enjoy dressing up in her mother's fancy clothes, donning her highest heels and clasping her elegant evening purses as we entered into an imaginary world where we were much older than our years. In those magical outfits we would become whoever we fancied and do whatever our dreams could conjure. Our imaginations were our only limit.

So it was with a twinge of fond reverie that I watched my youngest daughter mischievously slip into my most expensive pair of high heels. From a distance I watched her wobbling clumsily, attempting to find her balance. She looked as though she might topple over at any moment.

Just then, her younger brother entered the room. Seeing him, my daughter assumed my most authoritative tone of voice and began to instruct him as though she were myself. With her back upright, shoulders steady, and head held high, she looked as though the shoes were made for her, even though her small feet were inches short of reaching the heel end of the shoes.

The scene brought to mind the times in my life when I had been thrown into a position in which I felt like a little kid caught wearing her mother's high-heeled shoes. I, too, first wobbled clumsily in search of some balance, teetering on a platform too high for my own comfort.

Take, for example, the first time I was asked to deliver a formal talk to a gathering of women, each at least a decade older than my tender teen years. Almost shaking with fright as I prepared to leave home, I bumped into my father, who perceived just how unnerved I was.

He looked at me penetratingly and said just a few words — words that would become my mantra whenever I was faced with a load that looked too large or burdensome for my slight shoulders to carry. "Remember who and what you are," he stated simply before patting me on the shoulder, eyes smiling.

I took those words with me and repeated them over and over as I drove to that lecture and to many future lectures or situations where I felt like I was carrying too heavy a burden.

Standing before the crowd that night, feeling like I was wearing my mother's shoes, I did exactly what my youngster was doing now. I acted the part. And with the act came the poise, posture, and confidence — and even, surprisingly, the steady voice.

Because "remembering who and what you are" isn't about you, personally, at all. It isn't about wearing shoes that don't fit. It is, rather, about wearing shoes that represent all that you have, can, and will be.

Because what and who each of us is, is something far greater than we are aware.

Realizing "who and what you are" is realizing the potential within yourself and remembering the long chain of history that each of us carries. It is remembering the privilege and responsibility of a rich past leading into our present and future.

~ *When we recognize who and what we represent — along with all our vast potential — and act upon these possibilities, we become that person.*

These journal questions reflect values from the stories you just read. Record your answers for a greater awareness of your spiritual perspective on life.

On Potential
JOURNAL

1. Identify three things you feel passionate about.

2. How have you used your passion or ideals to assist another person?

3. Identify three of your positive qualities.

4. List three of your talents.

5. Identify one thing that is broken in your life. What steps are you taking to mend it?

6. Describe a situation where you helped someone and, in the process, gained immensely.

7. Describe a situation where you found courage that you weren't aware you possessed. What helped you to tap into this courage?

8. How can you generate more enthusiasm in any one area of your life?

II. Values and Perspective

ON HARDSHIP AND EXILE
ON EMPATHY
ON POSITIVE THINKING
ON PRIORITIES
ON THE POWER OF DEED

Chassidim would say:

*"Blow on a match and it becomes extinguished.
Blow on a hot coal and it bursts into a flame."*

*Don't allow hardships or challenges
to extinguish your spirit.*

Use these experiences to develop your latent potential.

On Hardship and Exile

Timed Out

No matter how determined I am, it happens every time. My little three-year-old will have done some misdeed, as mischievous three-year-olds do. He may have crayoned on the wall again despite having been warned about this several times or pulled his sister's ponytail really hard or refused to share his toys with one of his playmates. For any of these, he earns his "consequence" — three minutes of "time-out," as advised by the experts, one minute per year of age.

He'll sit on the designated step. Not even a half a minute will have passed when he'll approach me, blue eyes wide and intent, and mouth those magical words that melt a mother's heart.

"I'm sorry. Can I come out now? I won't do it again."

Of course, I am aware that within the hour he will repeat the same — or worse — misdeed. Nevertheless, I am also aware that for that singular moment his apology is sincere, his resolution real and his request heartfelt. So how can I deny him?

Sure, I may remain resolute the first time he asks and have him stay long enough to at least serve almost half of his three-minute sentence, but eventually I'll succumb to his pleas.

After all, we all make mistakes. The point is to learn from one's follies. Who's to say that the extra minute and a half would impart the lesson better? Besides, don't I want to teach him, too, the equally valuable lesson of forgiveness? Moreover, I just can't bear to see his face, so full of hope, fall as a result of my own doing.

Every mother knows this. Every mother has experienced it with her children.

And that's when I wonder about You, G-d. I think about how long Your "time-out" of exile has lasted. Don't You see our sad eyes raised to You? Don't You hear our apologies for our misdeeds? Don't You see our faces full of hope? Why must we be sent back, time and again, to finish serving our agonizingly long "time-out"?

Then I tell myself, *Maybe exile is not like that at all.*

Maybe it is more like me watching my six-year-old learn how to ride her bike without its training wheels.

I hold myself back, watching her try, again and again. I brace myself for the moment that I will let her go beyond my secure hold. Sadly, I watch her tip over. But as she falls and scrapes her knee against the hard concrete, I usher her into my arms and wipe away her tears. Eventually, if frustration overtakes her, I insist that we've practiced enough for now. Her feelings of failure are not worth the gain of the skill, and we can try again a different time when her self-image won't be so tarnished.

Then I wonder about You, G-d. Why, after our falls, don't we always feel Your warm embrace? Why don't our tears feel like they are being wiped away? And if we aren't acquiring whatever skill is intended, then is the growth really worth the pain?

At that point, I think perhaps exile is more like me insisting that my eleven-year-old clean her room. I'll tell her to go back, time and time again, until I know that she'll experience the pride and satisfaction of a job perfectly done.

But even then I'll monitor her reactions ever so carefully. I know that there is a fine balance between pride in earning something through one's own efforts and losing interest in it altogether.

So I may help her along or get her started in tidying up. I'll do whatever it takes to make sure that she doesn't despair, because I know full well that when she feels powerless, her efforts will be, too.

Then I wonder about You, G-d. I ponder why You allow us to feel so powerless. True, we will feel such pride in earning our redemption, but aren't You risking that we lose interest in it altogether?

I don't know which analogy to the various stages of my children's life is more precise. I'm not sure whether exile is a consequence meant to impart a lesson, like my three-year-old's time-out, or a learning experience to gain a new skill or awareness, like my daughter's bike lesson, or a refinement process that is self-earned, like cleaning up a room. Or maybe it is a combination of all of these.

But one thing is clear to me: I am certain that at some point, You, too, have a breaking point. Be it our tears, our frustrations, the tarnishing of our self-image, or our sincere longing and hope, at some point, I know that You also will decide enough is enough.

I just plead that You allow Yourself very soon to get to that point.

❧ *While realizing that hardships are meant to be learning experiences, G-d still wants to hear us ask to be better connected to Him.*

Potpourri

The trend in home furnishings nowadays is toward a homier, earthy décor. Softer lines, earth tones, real wood, and a back-to-basics approach contribute to a warmer and cozier home atmosphere. Home accessories, too, follow this pattern, as wicker baskets, fragrant candles, inviting plants, and patterned quilts or throw pillows abound.

Potpourri has become a popular outgrowth of this trend. Aisles upon aisles of home décor stores are filled with containers of varying shapes, hues, and fragrances of potpourri. Bags of spiced leaves or chips of aromatic wood mixed with dried fruit combinations emit an alluring earthy scent.

Lining the shelves as well is a whole array of containers to hold the potpourri. There are enough shapes, sizes, and materials – from glass, crystal, wrought iron, wood, and more – to please every discerning eye. Bring the potpourri into your home, and the aroma is instant. Open up those bags, and you've unleashed a nostalgic fragrance of the best that nature has to offer.

So, deciding to spice up my home in the midst of a gloomy, cloudy, and endless winter, I bought some potpourri. A small investment, I figured, to bring some nature inside when the surrounding outdoors was bare and desolate.

I arranged the combinations in strategic locations throughout my home and was instantly rewarded with the scent of rustic nature. Several of my children commented on how nice the smell was. My youngest, in particular, was entranced by the combination of color and aroma and pressed his little nose up against the leaves.

It happened slowly. So slowly, in fact, that we almost didn't notice. But a couple of weeks later, during my routine morning tidying, with my youngster following at my heels, I realized that the fragrance had faded. In fact, it was almost entirely gone.

As if on cue, my four-year-old asked, "Why don't the leaves smell anymore like they used to?"

"I have an idea," I suggested. "Let's try to shake them up. Then I think they'll smell again."

The two of us went around our house poking and rubbing the contents of the containers. To our satisfaction, the more we poked and shook the leaves, the more of the original outdoor aroma returned to our home.

"Why does the smell come back when we rub it?" my son inquired.

"Well, the smell is inside the leaves, but it only comes out when you rub," I explained. "It's like a rose," I continued. "Do you know why the rosebush has thorns?"

He shook his head, eyes focused on me intently.

"The rose grows among the thorns so that the thorns rub against it. When they rub it, its fragrance emerges — just like the potpourri."

Walking around with my child, I realized something integral from these simple containers of potpourri.

Every individual has an exotic aroma of potential within. Each of us is a potpourri combination, made up of unique qualities and traits. But there is nothing in life that does not require constant maintenance. We, too, require regular effort to exude the best of our person-alities, talents, and characteristics.

Moreover, sometimes it's the pokes, thorns, and shakeups which life so suddenly — and disturbingly — throws at us that bring out the best in each of us.

 ❧ *As life's circumstances shake you up, keep a mental picture of your-self as the captivating rose, exuding a breathtaking fragrance — pre-cisely because of the thorns that life offers you.*

Sending a Child Away

This morning I sent my son off to yeshivah.

He is my oldest son who turned thirteen only a few months ago. He will be boarding in the yeshivah dormitory, where the boys are allowed to return home for Shabbat once every few weeks.

My rational mind knows that this is the best place for my son to be at this stage of his life, where he will learn and absorb Torah values as he studies. But inside, I am feeling chaos.

My motherly instinct complains that he is so young and vulnerable, that he still needs his home and the pampering that only a mother can give.

My rational mind reassures me that the yeshivah grounds are only a short drive from my home. I can visit him whenever I please and check up on him and his progress.

But my motherly instinct has my stomach tied up in a knot of anxiety, the likes of which I haven't experienced since that moment I waved goodbye to my own parents as a youngster leaving for a month-long stay in overnight camp.

My rational mind understands that this is how my son will become the person I want him to be, the person he himself wants to be. That he is reaching toward independence in a warm environment that will nurture his spirituality.

But my motherly instinct asks: Will he like the food they serve? Will he sleep well at night? Are the beds comfortable?

My rational mind counters that these are insignificant trivialities compared to the benefits that he is sure to accrue.

But my motherly instinct questions: How often will he call home? Will I become a stranger to his thoughts and moods? Will I still be intimately involved in his growing up?

My rational mind says that he is on a new path of intellectual and spiritual discovery, surrounded by supportive teachers and friends. On his thirteenth birthday, he reached an apex, assuming the responsibilities of manhood, which he is proceeding to fulfill in the best possible manner.

But my motherly self walks past his bedroom, now quiet and bereft, and recalls how, what seems like only yesterday, I rocked his tender, tiny body in my arms. As I set the Shabbat table, a lump forms in my throat as I bypass his regular place setting, just to the right of his father's.

My rational mind tells me that I must let go so he can develop fully.

But my motherly instinct insists that I can, and should, be a full part of that development.

Today is a hard day for me. The two divergent selves within me are creating turmoil within as each voices its independent and true position.

I am convinced that there must be some way and some place to reach a harmony between the two. A blend of independent growth and dependent love; a fusion of the rational mind and the emotional motherly instinct.

I am convinced that there will come a time and a place when growth need not be intertwined with hardship. When an ascent need not be accompanied by a preceding descent.

I think of the exile of our soul from its heavenly abode next to our Father in Heaven. I hear her voice crying as she descends to the corporeality of our physical world, even while she is convinced of the importance and the merit of this descent. I hear her crying in loneliness and bitterness even while she perceives how this strange and faraway world is the very place where she can make an impact and accomplish her mission.

I hear the Shechinah's weeping voice descending with us to the depths of pain and misery even while being aware that this will bring the ultimate growth and refinement to our people and our world.

And I hear the Shechinah crying bitterly for a way and a time when growth need not be accompanied by such pain. When independence can be fused with dependence. When challenges need not be accompanied with grief and tears. When the divine soul can feel at home in our material world. And when the physical and the spiritual can mesh in a perfect synthesis.

As the Shechinah weeps, I think of my own motherly self missing her child even as I know that this is where he belongs — until the dawn of that special time when opposites will coexist and mind and heart shall meet in harmony.

᠅ *Our world is a world of paradox. In the same moment that you experience profound grief or pain, realize that you are growing from enduring its challenges.*

Reality Check

My mother was born with a green thumb. Her home overflows with large plants and flowers. She intuitively senses just how much to water a plant, in what type of soil it will prosper, when it is becoming diseased, and what treatment it then requires.

Growing up amid all this budding greenery, I, too, learned to appreciate how a plant can brighten even the dullest corners of a room, especially in the barrenness of our Canadian winters.

Unfortunately, though, I wasn't blessed with my mother's talent.

My mother will often present me with one of her many attractive plants. She'll painstakingly instruct me on watering and preferred location. But, try as I might, a few weeks after I've optimistically welcomed this new addition to my home, its leaves will invariably begin to droop and wilt. Before long, the once glowing plant is surrounded by a gathering puddle of fallen and dead leaves.

I'll return the plant, on its last leg of life, to my mother for resuscitation. Sure enough, after a few weeks under her tender care, the plant will return to its pristine condition, in full and gracious bloom.

She'll offer me another of her many burgeoning plants, this time one that requires less care and fastidiousness.

But the process will repeat itself, and has repeated itself so many times, that I finally became loath to continue my near murders. I became resigned that my huge southern-facing window – the perfect setting for almost any plant – would remain empty of growing things.

Instead, I opted for a more practical alternative. I searched the stores until I came across authentic-looking artificial plants.

Now a striking, tropical palm tree (my favorite tree) graces my living-room window and a large, fifteen-foot banana tree fills another corner. I now no longer need to feel guilty about forgetting the weekly watering or otherwise neglecting an innocent plant to death.

The other day my mother once again offered me a plant. She was grafting her very large cactus tree, which was getting too tall and wide to fit in her home.

"Don't worry, Chana," she reassured me. "The cactus plant will survive in almost impossible conditions. It needs almost no attention and only a scarce amount of water."

Reluctantly, I took it home for yet another attempt. Weeks have passed and the cactus is alive. In fact, it has grown and seems to be flourishing – as much as a cactus plant can flourish.

My husband wasn't particularly enamored with this latest addition. "You have so much lovely greenery. Why the need for this ugly thing?" he wondered aloud.

I stubbornly insisted that as long as the cactus plant continues to grow and live, it remains in our home. For, as exquisite as the other trees appear, they lack one essential and integral quality. They aren't real. They aren't alive. The cactus, with its bare thorns and irregular beauty, to me represents a life that is vibrant – pricks and all.

A thing that is alive, no matter how prickly or apparently unattractive, grows and develops. Regardless of our deficiencies, difficulties, and sufferings, the beauty, contribution, and realism contained by each of our lives is incomparably more beautiful than any artificial imitation of life could ever be.

And that's what I see in the cactus that commands center stage in my front window.

    ❧ *Life is a precious gift – despite its pricks and difficulties.*

Worth the Wrinkles

We finally did it.

We escaped from the city for a glorious four days of family vacation. We stayed in a small cabin, the dense forest behind us and the open meadow before us, surrounded by looming mountains and towering trees. Hiking trails crossing the paths of wild deer, ostriches, rabbits, and raccoons led to picturesque lakes and waterfalls. Add to that a swimming pool and a host of new friends for my children to play with, and this was a vacation everyone was enjoying.

I sat in the meadow, sun beaming, pen and paper in hand, as the children played happily around me. For once, I could think in calm silence and write to my heart's content instead of stealing a harried moment from the chores or responsibilities of my daily grind.

I sat, pen and paper in hand. But nothing emerged. My mind, usually bombarded with ideas, was as blank as the paper I was holding.

I attempted to write down a thought that had occurred to me earlier that week, to no avail. The words didn't flow. The sentences sounded forced.

Why? Why, when I had no pressures, no anxiety, no chores or responsibilities, no phone calls or people requiring my attention, was I so uninspired?

Only later did it occur to me that perhaps it is precisely those pressures, precisely those chores and responsibilities, precisely those tasks and people pulling me from all directions, that contributed to who and what I am and what I have to say.

Perhaps, like the character that is brought out only by the wrinkles on our faces and gray hairs on our heads marking our worries and our age, so, too, perception and insight will derive only from the bothers and burdens of daily living. Perhaps meaningful words can be set on paper only by a fully lived life, not one blank of responsibility.

I spent four glorious days luxuriating in the scenery, relishing the relaxation, experiencing nature and enjoying the time spent with my family – but my sheets of paper remained blank.

We arrived home from our vacation late on a Thursday night. Fridays are always busy days, particularly this one, after a four-day absence. I came back to deadlines, an incessantly ringing phone, a course syllabus to be published, a flight reservation to be booked – and, of course, all the hampers of laundry to be washed and folded, in addition to the usual Shabbat preparations.

And amid this all, when the pressures seemed their strongest, my mind was suddenly teeming with ideas and thoughts.

Maybe I'll even sneak a moment to record this one.

ॐ *Challenges, pressures, and responsibilities form us into fuller, wiser, and more complete human beings.*

Barren Beauty

Ever since I can remember, my husband's practice has been, like many men, to buy me a lovely bouquet of flowers for Shabbat. Tastefully he arranges them on the Shabbat table – his show of appreciation for the extra pre-Shabbat preparations and week-long exertions.

He never fails to delight me with his innovations. Sometimes it is an exotic bunch that I have never seen before, exuding an irresistible perfumed aroma. Other times it is the allure of the strikingly bold color coordination. Yet other times, it is the novelty of an artistic vase housing the brilliant bunch.

This past Shabbat was no different. As I rushed into the dining room to kindle the candles, just moments before the appointed time, I couldn't help but notice a captivating array adorning our table. This time, however, the arrangement was even more unique than any of its many predecessors.

About a dozen or more simple, thin, redwood branches stood elegantly in a narrow clay pitcher glazed to an olive-green, earthy tone. The branches were naked of any of their leaves or flowers, very much resembling the barren, wintry outdoors.

The arrangement was definitely distinct from the colorful blooms and leafy greens I and my children had become inured to.

And at first my children protested against having them on our Shabbat table.

But, looking at the mahogany-colored branches, I discerned a distinctive beauty, a certain essence, bereft of adornments, detached of scent, stripped of garments or presentation.

This was not the attractiveness of dazzling flowers or the thick foliage of blooming trees standing in their full height and glory, exulting in a sun's bathing rays, surrounded by chirping birds and children merrily and boisterously playing. This was, rather, the exquisiteness of a barren, winter day, of a gray horizon surrounding raw trees in a vast, empty landscape trapped beneath layers of white icy snow.

It symbolized the splendor found within the desolate, dark period of our lives, in the wonder of finding ourselves and exposing our potential — within our hardships and our pains.

It was a steadfast, veiled beauty that would not wilt with the decaying rosebuds nor evaporate with the flaccid, spicy leaves — like the successes of our lives which become obsolete with the passages of time.

My children found it difficult to appreciate.

"Are you really planning to keep this?" my youngsters queried at the end of Shabbat as they noticed me placing the branches as an artsy keepsake on the side table of our living room.

But I realize that this is a kind of beauty that takes the maturity and the experiences of living to recognize. Only after riding the ups and downs of the roller coaster we call the wheel of life, can one fathom beauty in the downs as well as the ups. Only after experiencing the immense barrenness of the desert can one perceive the dramatic charm in the grooves of its landscape.

To me, these dozen or so simple rosewood branches represented not the colorful, eye-catching charismatic beauty of doing, succeeding, and accomplishing but rather the simpler and stark, pristine purity of being and living.

    ❧ *Even within the stark evenings of life, appreciate the joy and beauty of being alive.*

G-d in the Laundry Room

My oldest daughter returned home late last night after having been away for two months at sleepover camp. On my mind now is what is on every mother's mind when her child returns from camp.

Yes, of course, I am thrilled that she is back. I know that over the next few days we will stay up into the late hours of the night catching up on all her experiences and adventures. Snuggled up on the couch over hot chocolate or tea, I will eagerly listen to her share and reminisce as she fills me in on all her new friends.

But, no, that is not what occupies my thoughts at this moment.

And, yes, of course, the fleeting thought has crossed my mind that now my in-house babysitter and righthand helper has returned. Yes, I considered how now, once again, I will be able to take up my late-night strolls with my husband or accept invitations to affairs at a moment's notice.

But, no, that, too, is not on my mind right now.

I am thinking of something far more mundane — what every mother thinks about with the return of her child from sleepover camp.

Laundry.

Loads and loads of it.

All the suitcases and duffel bags, still unpacked, have been directed straight to the laundry room. Load after load of whites and darks. Heavily soiled and lightly soiled. Delicate wear and regular cycles.

So I stand, engulfed by the piles on the laundry room floor neatly grouped according to task, water temperature, and degree of soil.

And I wonder about Your laundry. Do You, too, have different piles of missions and goals that you allot to different individuals? Do You group Your loads based on respective talents and capabilities? Do You, too, choose the varying life temperatures, the alternate degrees of ruggedness or gentleness, according to Your creatures' cares and needs?

The washing machine whirs incessantly. Around and around it agitates. Stopping here, adding water, rinsing, and spinning. Nonstop motion. At times the endless movement seems like pointless repetition. But eventually I see the laundry exiting, clean and fresh.

And I think of the many aspects of life that seem pointless. Do You ever watch the constant motion and wonder at the necessity of the repetition? Sometimes, only the power of hindsight clues us in on the purpose of life's turns. Sometimes, even that is lacking. Often, all we have is our trust in You that ultimately everything is for a purpose and our lives and world will emerge clean.

Then there are those clothes that are so stained or soiled that they require extra treatment. There are the whites that only return to their sparkling whiteness with the addition of strong bleach. There's the deeply ingrained soil that needs to be rubbed and scrubbed with harsh cleansers to erase their stains.

I cringe as I think of Your bottles of bleach and Your containers of harsh cleansers. I think of the brushes that You use to scrub us. I wince as I think of the many trials, tribulations, and challenges that You use to purify, refine, and teach us.

And then, once the laundry has been cleaned, dried, and folded, there is the special-wear clothing. Those blouses or shirts that get the extra care, reserved for special occasions, when we want to look our absolute best. For those, I spray starch on the collars, and I take out the hot iron to press hard against any creases or folds.

I ponder the special people around me who seem to be pressed continuously by Your hot iron. Yet the only crease on their faces is their ever-present smiles. I think about their perpetual words of comfort for others, despite their own predicaments. And I imagine You personally and affectionately tending to them.

So the task is completed. I can finally sit down to relax. With great effort, the loads of laundry have been washed, dried, folded, and put away.

Just as I am thinking that the workload has finally ended, I hear it — a new piece of laundry being dropped into the hamper.

There is still what to do.

᪣ *Life, like the laundry machine, sometimes whirs incessantly and feels pointless. But life's monotonous turns, harsh cleansers, and hot-iron situations help us emerge clean, refined, and at our very best.*

These journal questions reflect values from the stories you just read. Record your answers for a greater awareness of your spiritual perspective on life.

On Hardship and Exile
JOURNAL

1. What are some challenges or difficult situations that you have encountered over the last few years?

2. In retrospect, how have you grown from those situations?

3. List three positive qualities that you have acquired due to a challenge.

4. Describe a situation where helping another person required you to use "tough love." How did you feel?

5. What does exile mean to you?

6. Do you feel you are growing as a person? How?

7. Describe a situation where you had to step into an intimidating role. How did you successfully rise to the challenge?

On Empathy

The Uncelebrated Bar Mitzvah

My daughters and I had almost finished curling the gold and purple ribbons to be used on the centerpieces for my son Aharon's upcoming bar mitzvah, just four days away. I put the material aside. It could wait for when I returned a few hours later. Now I needed to rush off to my institute to coordinate the Sunday evening educational courses...

❧ ❧

Gently I closed the doors to one of the classrooms, just as the instructor began expertly leading the participants in their Basic Hebrew course. Having a few moments to spare before the next course on Jewish philosophy would begin, I decided to treat myself to a well-deserved tea break, which would warm me on this cold winter evening.

Nursing my steaming cup, I noticed a young boy just leaving from the shul sanctuary after having hesitatingly uttered foreign words of prayer. A woman to whom I was talking whispered in a hushed undertone how the boy's father had just died. An accident... On the highway... My heart sank and the tea turned cold inside me.

He had big brown eyes, a thick gold chain around his neck, an olive complexion and cherubic, round cheeks. He glanced at me. I wasn't sure whether to speak or remain silent, but my heart told me that I had to say something.

I made an attempt to reach out to those innocent brown eyes. "You said the prayers beautifully. I'm sure your father is very proud."

"Thank you," he replied genuinely as he turned away. Then he walked back a few steps toward me. "Do you know what happened?" he queried.

"No," I answered honestly. "Can you tell me?"

"He was on the highway. He was a truck driver. It was icy. Invisible, black ice. And snowing. The car ahead was stalled, needed help. My dad stopped, got out of his truck, and went to see what he could do. Another car drove by. The driver didn't see him. My dad was killed instantly. No one else was hurt. Some scratches and minor injuries, but nothing serious. He was the only one killed. Killed while helping another human being."

He said it all in a sad, matter-of-fact manner. I wished I could reach out and hug him.

"When did it happen?" I asked.

"A week and a half ago. On Wednesday. At 8:13 p.m."

"You sat shivah?"

"Yes. We got up a few days ago."

"How's your mom doing?"

"She's sad. Crying. Angry. It's very confusing."

"I'm sure," I empathized, though I wasn't sure at all of the pain they must be feeling. "Do you have any other siblings?" I inquired.

"Yes." He seemed to want to talk. "A sister, a little older than me."

"And how old are you?"

"Twelve. In another month I'll be turning thirteen. I was supposed to have my bar mitzvah." He paused. "But now I don't think I'll have my party anymore."

My heart sank further as I mumbled some words of encouragement. Something halfhearted about him being a source of *nachas*, Jewish pride, to his father. Something about him doing good deeds in his father's merit. Something about the beauty of dying while helping another individual. I encouraged him to be strong.

He nodded solemnly. Again I felt like hugging him, embracing him, and taking away the sadness from those young, tender eyes. He thanked me and left.

Just a few seconds on a highway that would make such a difference. A moment that changed the direction of a young child's life.

What different celebrations awaited my son and this boy.

What was the lesson of this "chance meeting"?

Honestly, I didn't really know. Perhaps it was meant to focus me on the real meaning of life. Not to get hung up on purple and gold ribbons. Perhaps it was to make me realize that I should count my blessings and appreciate all the good fortune that G-d constantly showers on me.

And perhaps it was meant to teach me to use an opportunity, the joyous occasion of my son's bar mitzvah, to say a silent prayer for this orphan boy, about to celebrate his own bar mitzvah — very differently than he had anticipated.

And to say a prayer for all orphaned boys and girls.

Perhaps to remind me to look up to G-d and ask Him, accuse Him, beg Him, demand of Him, "Dear G-d, how long must Your people suffer so?!"

So that the beautiful, big, dark eyes of this young boy — and all others like him — can smile in genuine happiness.

> ✧ *When witnessing another's grief, use the opportunity for empathy, action, self-evaluation, and gratitude.*
> *Empathize and do what you can to help.*
> *Evaluate whether your priorities are in order.*
> *And feel gratitude for all the good in your life.*

Baby-Sized Ego

She flagrantly disregards all rules of etiquette, defying the most commonly accepted social mores. She'll make noise when silence is expected. She'll laugh out loud when hushed reverence is called for. She'll eat noisily and messily, slurping down her meals, grunting loudly in appreciation of the foods she relishes and openly balking at those she does not.

Nor does she have any concept of respecting private space. She'll stick her face right into mine. My nose, glasses, and hair all become targets for her hands to grab onto.

She'll stare at complete strangers, maintaining eye contact with her wide-eyed gawk until her curiosity has been thoroughly satisfied. She has no concept of "waiting your turn." She'll interrupt my conversations to demand whatever it is she wants — and will persevere until she gets it — without the slightest apology or bashfulness.

Yet, despite her total lack of propriety, she's loved by all.

Grim-faced strangers will approach her in the street to smile at her. Mature adults will make all sorts of silly faces and witless gestures for the gratification of her laugh.

My older children may come home from school in a cross mood, snapping at whomever they encounter to express their frustration. But put them in a quiet room with her, and they become almost miraculously transformed. Their talk becomes gentle, their gestures loving.

☙ ❧

"She" is my six-month-old baby.

What is it about a baby that is so charismatic? What is the secret to her charm? Why do we not only tolerate a baby's disregard for social norms and her invasion of our personal space — but even enjoy it?

Many things draw us to babies: their purity and innocence, their vulnerability and need for protection, their trust and optimism — things that our burdened, older selves have long ago discarded. And, of course, there is simply the baby's adorable cuteness. But I think that the true source of a baby's allure is her complete lack of self-consciousness. Her almost egoless state of being.

Now here's where you'll object and tell me that a baby has the biggest ego there is. All she knows is one big "I." She screams and demands her needs, completely oblivious to the fact that there are others in this world besides her who are worthy of consideration.

This is true. A baby is intuitively convinced of her own importance. She is also conscious of the admiring stares of those around her and thrives on them.

But a baby's sense of selfhood is an honest, altruistic one. She will assert herself purely for its own sake, not for any ulterior motive. She will clamor for her needs in the best ways she knows, but she is not making a statement through them. Her needs are simply her needs, not a way of demanding attention or respect or of asserting control over others.

It is true that she has not yet discovered social mores — those laws and rules meant to teach us consideration in living together with others. But, by the same token, these rules all too often also dictate a lifelong pursuit of trying to make ourselves into someone else — into others' perceptions of what we should ideally become — rather than having the courage to discover who we truly are.

A baby is infatuated with everything around her. She is engaged in a perpetual quest to decipher and manipulate her surroundings, to learn how she can be a part of it — but without any need to control or subdue it.

Often, when we assert our "I," it's not a matter of our real, or even perceived, needs and wants. It is more an issue of my "I" competing for space with your "I." When I want something, it's often because you have it, so why should I do without? Why should I command less respect or control than you do?

Our zealous protection of "personal space" is also often a matter of this battle of the I's. The story is told of a chassid who once came to his Rebbe, Rabbi Menachem Mendel, the third Chabad Rebbe, complaining that "everyone is stepping on me" — forever interfering with his sphere of influence or involving themselves in his affairs.

Answered the Rebbe: "If you wouldn't spread yourself all over the place, there would be room for others, too, and they wouldn't need to step on you wherever they go."

We feel the need for personal space when there is too much of another's "I" interfering with our own. When my "I" is so unbending and full of my sense of entitlement, I fail to make room for your likewise strong sense of "I" and become uncomfortable being in too close proximity with it.

We think we are asserting ourselves by demanding that our "I" be heard. In truth, we are pursuing an "I" that is the artifact of our societal machinations, rather than the inner "I" of our real and true calling.

A baby, in contrast, introduces us to refreshingly honest and natural selfhood. When she makes her presence known or clamors for her needs, she's not using these as a cover for any hidden agenda. When she smiles at you, she's not out to be a master over you or to subdue you. She's not even interested in entertaining you or making you feel good. She merely is what she is. Without any apology. Without any self-consciousness. Without any personal agenda. Without any arrogance. Without seeking anyone's approval.

And that is what we love so much about her.

So much, in fact, that we're even willing to let her pull at our noses.

ᔓ *Making "room" for another in your life means feeling less of a sense of personal entitlement and more of an awareness of the needs of another.*

In Love's Reflection

"Now I'm too big to hug you," my five-year-old son, Yisroel, announced somewhat uncertainly as he observed me nursing my newborn baby soon after I returned home from the hospital.

"No, honey, you can still hug me," I assured him, making room for him next to me.

Smiling broadly, he climbed onto my bed and explained to me, "It's not that I don't want to hug you. I just thought that now I was too old for that."

After this insightful remark, I made a mental note to be extra cautious to include Yisroel any time I was with my baby, Sara Leah. Having a new baby was a big change for all of us. But being the youngest for so many years, this transition was hardest on him. I also began to tell Yisroel how much Sara Leah loves him and would grow to love him even more as she got older.

My children often heard me remark how with each new sibling I was giving them the best gift ever. Siblings are the gift of a special bond that remains for life, wherever one lives and however life treats you.

"You'll always be Sara Leah's BIG brother. She'll adore you and learn so many things from you," I now inform Yisroel.

He seemed to relate to this concept since he was in awe of his older siblings, especially his older brother Aharon, who, ten years his senior, would teach him new tricks.

A few weeks later, when Sara Leah began smiling, Yisroel was convinced (with a little encouragement from the rest of us) that she loved him the most from the whole family.

"She smiles the biggest smiles to *me*," he proudly proclaimed, watching her grin.

Nevertheless, I still looked out for opportunities to bolster Yisroel's confidence. But Yisroel surprised me.

A few days later, I bumped into one of the mothers of Yisroel's classmates. While driving the boys' car pool, she had overheard their discussion. There had been a raging debate as her son Mendy and Yisroel both asserted that their baby deserved the coveted title of "cutest baby."

She found it particularly heartwarming to hear Mendy describe her two-year-old as the cutest, since her baby was born with Down's syndrome and required so much of her time away in therapy.

"Yisroel, however," she continued, "was unrelenting and was about to insist that all the boys come into your home to vote on his sister being the cutest!"

I pictured Yisroel adamantly insisting on his stance.

"Fortunately, the boys reached a compromise," she concluded. "They decided that Mendy's brother is the cutest 'boy baby' and Yisroel's sister is the cutest 'girl baby.'"

We both smiled at this ingenious resolution. Both of us were even more relieved at the affectionate feelings our children had acquired toward their younger siblings.

I remembered this short conversation as I was tucking in Yisroel at bedtime several nights later. He again surprised me by telling me that he had announced in school that he was the most loved.

"My family all love me," he told me he had confidently asserted. "And my baby loves me the most."

I nodded contentedly. "Yes, but how do you know that the baby loves you?"

"I love her so much because she's my baby sister," he replied, "so I know that she must love me so much, too!"

↬ *When we can begin to see someone as "ours," we no longer feel threatened by them. Moreover, another's love is a mirror reflection of our own.*

Experiencing Another: Prayers at the Ohel

The "Ohel," the resting place of the Lubavitcher Rebbe, is visited by many the world over. People from all walks of life and various levels of observance are drawn to pray at this holy site.

At the Ohel all suppressed emotions are allowed expression. So, unlike my usually reserved self, I stand in fervent, intense moments of prayer to pray for the many arenas of my life where blessing is so sorely needed. In the solemn silence, I hear my own soul speaking, searching, crying, and yearning. I complain from the depths of my being for all the negativity in the world, for all the pain and hardship, for all the reasons why the redemption is so vital.

I feel like a young child who is resting on his difficult journey at his familiar, cozy childhood home. Pausing from his long and arduous travels, he visits his kind and loving father, whose infinitely understanding eyes empathize with his hardships and lighten his load.

My own chest feels lighter, my searing wounds less painful, after receiving such a caressing, warm embrace of empathy and blessing. I can then return to my own life's journey, the burden somehow lightened, confident that my prayers will be answered, enriched by the spiritual connection.

This has always been my experience at the Ohel.

My tears flow freely as my whole body succumbs to prayer. Intermingled with spontaneous requests, sincere resolutions, strong demands, and the prepared texts of the prayer books, my lips move silently but incessantly.

My eldest daughter's eyes lock with mine, and at first she is alarmed. Esther is not accustomed to seeing her mother so painfully distraught, her wounds gushing so openly.

But after meeting my eyes again, her own prayers become more intense, her features more solemn — and then more serene — as she, too, learns the secret of facing her soul as she unburdens herself at the Ohel.

Suddenly, inexplicably, I search the faces of the others around me. In the usually crowded area, two stand out.

They have come together — an older man with a younger one. They appear to be related, perhaps father and son or father and son-in-law. They are praying in unison, crying bitterly, at times hysterically. It is apparent that they are confronting a critical situation, perhaps even a life-and-death matter. Their faces are strained; this is their last vestige of hope.

Coming face to face with the gravity of another's anguish, my own issues feel trivial. All my wants and needs, which but a moment before encompassed my very being, feel inconsequential.

I pause in reflection, contemplating their tormented expressions.

I find a greater earnestness in my prayers. What had been an endless list of my most pressing needs and wants is topped off with an added one.

And for that solitary moment, there only exists that one, embracing request.

Please, dear Rebbe, pray for these two individuals. Bless them that the misery and agony in their lives be eliminated. Pray that their pain be healed and that their prayers be answered.

And in that moment, one verse repeats itself over and over in my mind, as I beseech our Creator, "Bless us, our Father, all of us, as one!"

Prayer means reaching deep inside yourself. Only when you can experience the pain of another as your own pain have you reached deeply enough.

Face to Face

Ever have this feeling? You are in a room brimming with people and you feel absolutely alone.

I remember that feeling being so pronounced once when I was sitting at a table of acquaintances at a relative's bar mitzvah. It's not that I didn't know the people at my table. I did. It's not that the conversation wasn't flowing. It was. But though we were all talking amicably, we failed to really connect — and hence the feelings of aloneness.

Then there are times when I can be sitting at home with one of my children or my husband. We're each doing our own thing. But the connection is palpable, and none of us feels alone.

As humans we crave to feel connected, but there are natural barriers that prevent it. Each of us has his or her independent thoughts and his or her own sense of emotions — things that define who we are and make each of us a unique human being. But that is also what divides us.

Intuitively, we seek to unearth that spiritual bond between all of us, our inner connection as humans. If we fail to do so, we sense aloneness. It's not a loneliness, but rather an aloneness — a feeling that I and you haven't reached deeply enough to break external barriers.

Sometimes, though, we can unearth a connection even with complete strangers – even in a room packed with nameless strangers.

A couple of months ago, I organized a program at our institute. I had asked two women to speak about how they had coped with particularly challenging personal tragedies in their lives and discovered within themselves strength, courage, and inspiration. I knew that their talks would be raw, honest, and painful, but also inspirational and full of courage.

About a week before the program, I called a friend to invite her to join. I was taken aback by her response.

"Why would I want to attend? I have enough *tzaros* (suffering) in my life! Why should I become more upset by hearing about someone else's?"

Throughout that week, I thought about my friend's response. I wondered if I was mistaken in choosing such a topic. But I was pleasantly relieved to see an overflow audience, with every available seat occupied.

Our first speaker, Chavi, spoke about how two years ago to that week, her husband had been killed by a crazed murderer on a quiet Toronto street. It had been a month before their twenty-fifth anniversary when her husband had gone out, on his birthday, to help her son a few blocks away with a flat tire. The killer shouted at her husband for being a Jew before plunging in the knife, instantly killing him.

The newspapers at the time were flooded with the news. Chavi explained how that tragic moment affected her and her six children personally. The knife that snuffed out her husband's life shattered all their dreams and hopes for a beautiful shared future.

But through the horror she knew she had to become an example for her children in finding the courage to be all that their father would have wanted them to be, with their heads held high. Nothing was obvious in her search for meaning and faith. She had to redefine who she was personally and find a courage she didn't believe she possessed – for herself and for her children.

The next speaker, Orna, is a mother whose son at the age of two choked on a grape. He was rushed to the hospital where he was miraculously revived and eventually began breathing on his own, but remains to this date — several years later — comatose.

Orna described how she fiercely fought with the hospital doctor who wanted her to pull the plug and "let G-d decide the outcome." Despite the horror of her situation, she bravely replied to him, "We are partners with G-d, and He wants us to do our part."

In a moment of utter honesty, Orna confessed, "I would never choose the life that I have been given. But through it all, I have been transformed so that I like the 'I' that I am today better than the 'I' that I was yesterday."

Both of these courageous women received a standing ovation for their talks. By the time the evening was over, there were very few dry eyes in the audience.

The warm reception was proof enough that as humans we want to connect in the deepest way possible. We want to hear and experience what another is feeling. Sometimes, unfortunately, that only comes out through feeling another's pain and suffering.

My friend's comments had originally bothered me, but now I had found a response.

As the master of ceremonies for the evening, I also spoke. I explained that there was a lesson behind G-d's voice emanating from between the *keruvim* (cherubim), which were carved in the image of two faces turned toward each other.

"G-d is teaching us the importance of looking into another person's face — into another's heart and soul — and experiencing a real connection. Sometimes, when we look into another's heart, we see and share joy, smiles, laughter, and happiness. We enjoy such experiences.

"And sometimes, when we look into the heart and soul of another, we see pain, tears, and suffering. We don't enjoy these experiences. It makes us feel sad, tearful. We want to hide from such encounters. But facing such encounters, too, is what being alive and being human is all about.

"And, as we find room in ourselves to look into another's heart and soul and experience the depths of their happiness and joy – or their sadness and pain – that is precisely where we will find the voice of G-d."

    ❧ *Bonding with another means being willing to share with them – and help them through – their joy as well as their pain.*

Making the Grade

The French are proud of their high couture and cuisine, the English have their fixation with propriety and political institutions, the Americans' greatest passion is their pop culture. And here, in Canada, we obsess over...the weather.

Rarely will a conversation pass without some mention of the weather. The weather makes the top headlines in the news and is broadcast several times a day. You can't blame us Canadians for this mania, living as we do in a country that experiences such extreme changes — from hot, humid summers to blistering cold, snow-filled winters.

On days when the sun shines, people's faces shine brightly as they express how happy the warmth makes them feel. And on days when the clouds loom dark above us, when the winds gust and the rainstorms pound the pavement, you'll hear conversations about headaches pounding on throbbing temples. Tempers will flare as the atmosphere becomes as dark and gloomy indoors as it is outdoors — all due, of course, to the weather.

After all, aren't we all products of our environment, allowing the outside atmosphere to permeate within?

Each of us has his days. There are days when I feel like the sun is smiling down on me. Just about everything is going right. My kids and husband are happy, generous, and loving. My car starts with hardly a purr and drives uneventfully through calm traffic. My friends call just to share a kind word, and strangers smile at me at the grocery checkout counter. If I'm really lucky, I'll even get a compliment from my boss at work.

I'm riding the clouds, exulting in the love and kindness around me. On these days, I smile inwardly and luxuriate in self-love.

Then there are days when everything seems to be going wrong. The dinner burns. My favorite outfit no longer fits properly. My creativity is stymied, my work unproductive. My children are complaining. And, to top it off, my car gets a flat tire.

On those days, I want to crawl into a corner and never come out. I feel like an empty, valueless thing. Any self-love or self-worth has utterly vanished.

Last week, on just such a day, my usually cheerful daughter came home from school completely despondent. Slowly and reluctantly, she pulled out a test paper from her knapsack and, with downcast eyes, asked me to sign it. She was trying to fold over her low grade, but I need not have even seen the crumpled paper. The sad look in her eyes told me more than any number on a paper could reveal.

Her grade made her feel like a valueless failure, not worthy of being loved.

Looking down at my precious daughter, understanding so well her inner turmoil, I wondered how I could convey to her that she was loved despite any failed endeavor. Being so intimately familiar with those feelings myself at the time, I knew how important it was for me to reach into her sad eyes and explain to her that she was worth so much more than red pen marks on a paper. That no event in her day – or in her life, for that matter – would take away from her intrinsic worth. That nothing would diminish who or what she was or how deserving of love she was.

Certainly I feel proud of her accomplishments when she succeeds. But that is pride, not love. Of course, I prod her to exert her greatest efforts and extend herself to her limits. But all that is only ways of finding expression for her talents and capabilities. None of her successes or failures increases or diminishes one iota of her intrinsic worth as a creation of G-d or the love that I will always unconditionally feel for her as my daughter.

And as I spoke to my precious daughter, I, too, realized that though it is up to us to try our best and exert ourselves to the utmost, no grade, no failing on our part, and no negative circumstance in our lives can ever affect our intrinsic worth as a beloved child of G-d.

Somehow, despite the dark clouds of our Canadian weather outdoors, I no longer felt any desire to crawl into a corner.

The room was filled with too much sunshine.

꙳ *Our essential worth is not dependent on any external events or accomplishments, but rather on what each of us is: a beloved child of G-d.*

That Extra Moment

I t was a typical end-of-the-year school play. I, like all the other mothers of this third-grade class, dutifully arrived at the school auditorium, prepared to feel awash with gratified pride. Our lips were pursed to smile unabashedly with de-light, our cameras set to flash endless pictures of our young daughters' performances.

Like a number of other mothers and grandmothers already present, we zealously arrived early to snap up a coveted front-row seat, to snatch a firsthand glimpse of our daughters, and to send confidence-building winks and smiles their way to allay any lingering pre-play stage fright.

As a grandmother of one of my daughter's friends, you were there, too, to share in this moment of joy. You were circulating around the room, passing by each row and extending a welcoming greeting. A smile passed over each face after you shared some pleasant or witty word of kindness.

I sat impatiently, waiting for the play to commence as I observed you finding something to say to so many people. Watching as you stopped by each and every chair, I surmised you must have many friends and were acquainted with many people.

Then you reached my chair. I didn't expect you to pause at all. After all, we didn't really know each other and only met infrequently on these rare school occasions.

So I was surprised that you did stop right in front of me. You made direct eye contact, and you politely exchanged some perfunctory comments. I was waiting for you to move on to someone you knew better, but instead you took an extra moment to find a point in common with me — me, a young mother, and you, a seasoned grandmother. You said that you knew my father well, and you told me what a beautiful person he was and how you saw the same inner beauty in my eyes.

It was almost a strange comment to say to a near stranger. Almost too serious and meaningful for such a chance encounter. Almost a ridiculous compliment, given the context.

Almost, but not really.

Somehow those few words spoken so genuinely touched me deeply and heartened me. I smiled like all the others to whom you spoke, inwardly encouraged.

Maybe some other day I would have regarded your comment as meaningless, almost silly, and certainly not worth a second thought. But not that day. On this day, it became engraved in my thoughts.

You see, just that morning, shortly before I arrived at the school play to enjoy the respite of an afternoon of motherly pleasure, I received a phone call. The call blackened my world and stole my cheer.

I was informed of the tragic news that medical tests that my father had recently undergone pointed to a large growth. The doctors' prognosis was grim.

It wouldn't be until several months later — after endless tears were shed, earnest communal prayers recited, and a harrowing surgical experience — that the miraculously benign growth was removed and my father recovered fully. But at that moment, after replacing the phone in its receiver, my worldview turned dismal.

I drove to my daughter's play trying to collect my thoughts as tears blurred my vision. It wouldn't be fair to burden my young and excited daughter with my emotions. Today was her special day. She had so eagerly anticipated proudly demonstrating the culmination of several weeks of preparation to her mother.

For her sake, I would have to withhold my intense feelings. I would have to put the grim news in the back recesses of my mind and, at least for these few hours of the afternoon, pretend that nothing had been disclosed to me.

The moment you approached me, I was trying desperately to remove any vestige of worry from my mind. I was trying to erase the creases of tension from my knotted forehead, to force my lips into a casual smile and focus my mind on the impending play. For my daughter's sake, I had to laugh at all the comical parts and clap when applause was called for, even if I heard and saw nothing but the vision of my father before my eyes. I told myself I could not and would not allow melancholy to overtake me — at least, not now.

As I felt the anguish of this mental wrestling, you approached me. You said your sweet words. Words that any other day may not have sounded nearly so appropriate or nearly so sweet. You had no idea how your sincere words were a pleasant distraction that comforted a mind racing with bleak thoughts.

When someone is in a difficult circumstance, when one's worldview becomes dark and oppressive, any smile, any kind word of encouragement, becomes a soothing balm — just as any harsh, critical words become that much more painful to endure.

Unbeknownst to you, you uplifted me on that day.

In retrospect, thinking about you making your rounds up and down the aisles, I could see that you did that for every person in the room. I don't know what emotional burden each of the other mothers and grandmothers was carrying, but I could witness their momentary encouragement as you passed by each of them.

We all carry some hurt, some struggle, some pain. Whether we choose to share it with others is our own valid choice. But a word of kindness from another — even a stranger — can penetrate to our psyche to slightly lighten our burden and temporarily brighten our demeanor.

    ∾ *Realize the power of your words. And then choose them more carefully.*

A Driving Lesson

I drove home from work on one uneventful sunny Tuesday afternoon, as I do every other day. The clock on my dashboard showed ten minutes before one. My youngest son usually arrives home from school with his car pool shortly after one o'clock, so I would have ample time to spare before he rushed through the front door, and even some extra minutes to take care of a small chore.

Instead, I found myself driving on the quiet side streets near my home trapped behind a student in a gray driver's training car. She drove slowly, *v-e-r-y* slowly, unbearably and painfully slowly. This was clearly her first experience on the road. Despite the deserted streets, she waited at every stop sign for what felt like an eternity, deliberately looking one way and then the other before proceeding. She drove much below the already low speed limit and at every bend in the road slowed down further still.

Usually I would be impatiently fuming about how this threw off my schedule by delaying me (by at least three extra minutes!). On any other day, I would have thoughtlessly swerved in front of this car and raced ahead to my destination.

But this afternoon, I didn't. Patiently, I drove the remaining distance to my home behind her. I didn't check the speedometer five times a minute to verify that she was still driving at least ten miles under the limit. Tolerantly, I waited by each stop sign as she checked to her right and to her left, though no cars were anywhere in sight. Considerately, I drove far behind her gray car, making sure not to tailgate even slightly so as not to unnerve her.

What was the source of this change in my mood this afternoon? Had I evolved into a more patient person? Or was I perhaps enjoying the suburban scenery along the route?

None of the above. The change in my perspective on this Tuesday afternoon was for an entirely different reason.

Just the day before my own sixteen-year-old daughter came home in just such a driver's training car. Excitedly, she entered our home and described to me her first adventure as a driver.

Always the ambitious one, she had taken her written test the day after her sixteenth birthday and now was able to drive a car with an instructor. She eagerly embraced this opportunity to demonstrate her responsibility and maturity.

Proudly I had watched her turn into our driveway, just yesterday, and observed her patiently and carefully looking to her right and to her left before proceeding.

So when I saw the student driving ahead of me in a similar car, I didn't see a nameless stranger. I could almost visualize my own daughter sitting beside her instructor. And suddenly, the few moments stolen from my day's schedule didn't matter at all.

When I was able to see my own child in that car, my perspective was completely transformed. I found all the patience in the world to allow her to enjoy her driving experience.

ℱ *When we can foster a feeling of empathy for another like we have for ourselves, our perspective changes entirely. Our world becomes a far more patient, more accepting – and better – place.*

These journal questions reflect values from the stories you just read. Record your answers for a greater awareness of your spiritual perspective on life.

On Empathy
JOURNAL

1. Identify five blessings in your life.

2. Describe a situation where you empathized with another human being. How did it make you feel?

3. Take time out of your day to express gratitude for the good in your life.

4. Share a gift of love with your most cherished person today.

5. Describe a friendship where you bonded through pain and through joy.

6. Describe how you have resolved a conflict in your relationship.

7. Think of an individual who has wronged you. Describe one special, positive quality of that individual.

8. Describe a situation where your choice of words could have been instrumental or detrimental. What helped you choose the right words?

On Positive Thinking

Frame of Mind

"These growths are often not malignant," my doctor said after examining me and looking through the results of the medical reports. "However, they can develop into malignancies. It is also uncommon to have, as you do, two growths. I would usually remove them as soon as possible." He paused. "Of course, being that you are four months pregnant, that limits our options."

The devastating news was beginning to sink in. I took a deep breath as he continued, "We could do an emergency operation. However, that would risk premature labor. Alternatively, we could wait until your sixth month, but although that would increase the chances of the baby surviving, it would mean the possible complications of a premature birth. Past the sixth month, I wouldn't recommend any operation."

Dr. Rosman glanced at me thoughtfully. "The other option, which is probably the best route, is to monitor you for any further enlargement and operate once the baby is born."

I nodded in agreement. Then he warned, "There is a danger that these growths may unexpectedly twist or erupt. You would feel a crushing pain. Rush immediately to the hospital. The pregnancy may be terminated.

"There is also the risk that they may grow very large. In that case, we would have to further determine our course of action. Think about these options and we'll speak further," Dr. Rosman concluded.

He was a caring and competent doctor who had done his best to convey the news sensitively. I tried to maintain a stoic expression as I left my doctor's office, but within I was absolutely shattered.

Driving the short distance home, I refused to release the torrent of tears just yet. Even tears, I was sure, would be unable to wash away the huge sickening feeling growing in the pit of my stomach.

Later that night, I finally permitted the tears to flow freely. As I tucked in my two younger children at bedtime, I relented. Listening to my young children's breathing grow softer and softer, and, gazing at their plump, tender, dimpled cheeks, I wondered if I would watch them grow into mature adults. The darkness of the room was my refuge that allowed me to vent my emotions and allowed my mind to consider the darkest, harshest possibilities.

On many more such nights I allowed myself to face the fears emerging from the darkest corridors of my being. During those nights, gazing at my children, I gained a new view on life, on my children, and on trying to keep a perspective on my priorities.

It took every fiber of strength and faith not to allow myself to become completely overpowered by the onslaught of haunting thoughts that never failed to terrify me, day or night, during those unforgettable months. Each night, as I lay in bed, I wondered if perhaps tonight I would be awakened by the unthinkable occurring.

Of course, my natural tendency to imagine the worst did not help. I had always been a worrier, preparing for the worst possible scenario.

My husband, on the other hand, was the optimist, who would try to clear my mind of its black outlook. At first I almost resented his attitude, wondering in half-seriousness, "Don't you even care about me? How can you speak with such optimism?" But as time progressed, I learned to appreciate his positive thinking and tried hard to incorporate it into my own.

I was fortunate as well to "coincidentally" come across and learn many teachings on faith, healing, and how positive thinking causes positive outcomes. These, as well as my husband's perspective, fortified me so that I could withstand those dark moments when my negativity cast a shadow over every arena of my life.

During these months of nervous anticipation, I whiled away my days, taking refuge in my work, my children, and my responsibilities. As the dean of a young women's seminary at the time, there was enough to become involved with to forget my personal troubles.

My students were never aware of the thoughts that passed through my mind every morning as I settled behind the closed doors of my office. Nor did they realize the reason for my intensity when I would teach them a discourse on faith. They never suspected the sickness or constant nausea that I felt or the gloom that penetrated my being. Nor did they suspect what a balm of spiritual healing the Torah teachings that I taught them brought to me.

During those difficult days I often thought how strange it was that one could be living in such close proximity with another, yet be totally unaware of what he may be facing. And worse, one may even be judging the other by one's own standards.

There are fortunate individuals who, when in distress, can reach out to others to gain the support they need. I, on the other hand, withdrew deep within myself.

I found it difficult to speak to my parents. My father would have been a natural choice for any other member of our community facing a similar situation. As the communal rabbi, he had given spiritual counseling and direction to so many others in similar circumstances, or worse. Yet to me, speaking to my father, or mother, was too painful. As a daughter, I observed what an outsider couldn't detect — the intense emotion on their faces, the lines of worry around their eyes. I discerned the subtle change in their voices that signified worlds to me.

With this intimate sense of their pain at watching their youngest child suffer, I found it unfair to burden them further by communicating my feelings or doubts. As a result, I avoided the topic almost entirely.

The months passed slowly.

Thank G-d, little Yisroel Pinchas was born a robust and healthy child in the late summer months without any complications. A new school year had begun, and with a newborn at hand, time went by in a blur of activity, too busy to even stop to contemplate. My surgery was scheduled, and I had hoped to recuperate quickly and be back in school, at least on a part-time basis, soon after.

Divine providence ordained differently. My strength was not sufficiently regained, and Dr. Rosman delayed the surgery several more months.

We scheduled it for the next seminary break, right before Chanukah. Dr. Rosman suggested that instead of conventional surgery, we should try a procedure whereby the growths could be removed through the insertion of a small needle. It would be less painful, recovery would be easier since scarring is much less, and I could be out of the hospital in one day. This sounded like a brighter option.

I was wheeled into the operating room with a prayer on my lips. Several hours later I awoke only to hear the news that I would soon be released.

Dr. Rosman had inserted the needle to withdraw the growth and probed the area. Miraculously the growth had vanished! For the first time in a year I could actually relax. An open miracle. No growth. It was gone.

For some reason, a nagging thought in the back of my mind still gnawed, but the euphoria of the moment silenced it.

Unfortunately, the miracle did not last more than a couple of months, when another test showed that the growths were indeed exactly where they had been. Strange as it was for the doctor not to have seen them, the problem remained.

I remember discovering at the time that though we make our own calculations or theories about why situations happen as they do, ultimately we are mere pawns in a greater Master Plan that is well beyond our control or comprehension. All we can do is accept that plan and have faith in it.

Spring was already in the air, a time usually reserved for rejuvenation and growth. I had a bouncing, adorable baby at home, but this dark cloud remained over my head. Surgery was scheduled for the summer months.

At the crack of dawn, my husband and I drove to the hospital. Waking while it was still dark and driving through the deserted streets made us feel like it was the morning before Yom Kippur, when we awaken early to do the *kapparot* ritual. I remember gazing at the blooming trees and contemplating how today would be my personal day of judgment.

My eyes brimmed with tears as I thought of my sleeping children. On each of their cherubic cheeks I had squarely planted a tender kiss earlier that morning. *For their sakes, dear G-d, make this successful,* I prayed.

I tried to be cheerful, but, of course, the mood was a solemn one. I could sense the lines of anxiety on my husband's features as he calmly reassured me that things would work out fine.

Preliminary testing had been completed, and I was wheeled to the waiting room. To calm our nerves and to occupy us with something spiritually constructive, we began learning Torah.

The discourse was discussing the mystical dimension of the oil used to light the Menorah in the Beit HaMikdash (Temple). The Torah describes it as "the oil of olives crushed to provide light." Just as the olive unleashes its oil by being crushed and squeezed, the highest levels of spiritual attainment are achieved through crushing pain and suffering.

The nurse came to wheel me into the operating room, and my husband smiled at me reassuringly. I tried hard to focus on the last words he had taught me, just as the oxygen mask descended over my face and my world went blank.

I don't remember much of the blur of the next few days in the hospital. I was on painkillers and groggy most of the time. But I do remember my immense relief in hearing that the growths that had been inside of me for so long had finally been removed. Both, thank G-d, had been benign, and several days later I was able to return home to my family.

Common wisdom asserts that hindsight is always perfect twenty-twenty vision. For over a year and a half, something negative, though benign, had cast a dark shadow on my life. What should have been a joyous time of pregnancy and birth became instead a time of terrible worry, anxiety, and fear, largely because I allowed it to be.

While this is, of course, easy to write in hindsight, it is also a lesson that I know I need to cultivate. Life is full of negative experiences – things that really don't belong and shouldn't be there to bother or upset us. Some of these experiences are more benign than others. But whatever the cause, and whatever the situation, how much we empower these circumstances to disturb the joy of our lives is largely our own decision.

୨ *You do not control circumstances, but your frame of mind is something that you yourself construct.*

Think Good, It Will Be Good!

Tomorrow is the day after Labor Day.

We all know what that means.

It's been looming large on our calendars for the last two months. Advertisements and flyer promotions have been announcing it for the last three weeks. "Back to School" signs are all over the place, signaling the first day of school.

This day represents the end of long and lazy summer days, the end of time being our own and the beginning of a tight and rigid schedule to last throughout the next ten months.

I know that my children will not sleep much tonight. As early as I send them off to bed to try to get in a good night's rest for the Big Day tomorrow, I know that they will remain awake, tossing and turning until finally a fitful sleep will mercifully overtake them. Their minds will be racing in nervous anticipation, just as mine did years ago before my own first days of the new school year. Those terrible tight knots in the pit of their stomachs are quite familiar to me.

Sure, excitement is part of their feelings. But mostly, they are feeling worried. Worried about how things will develop.

Will they have nice teachers? Will they be given too much homework? Will the social setting in their group change? Will their friends still be friendly after two months of being apart? Will the material from the new grade be difficult to learn? In which extracurricular activities will they take part? What can they do to make this year a better one?

These and a host of other questions will worry my children tonight as they lie open-eyed in bed, worry robbing them of their much-needed sleep.

So as my children are lying awake and worrying, I am thinking about worry.

I am thinking that it is very likely the worst possible emotion.

The only emotion even remotely as taxing is hopelessness. But while hopelessness is stressful, I think most of us can deal with it. When we realize that we are powerless to effect a situation, we surrender and submit to the fact that this is how it must be. And we adapt ourselves to our circumstances as best as we are able.

The problem arises, however, when we have a gnawing doubt that maybe we can do something to alter the situation. That doubt can ravage us within as our mind is in a quandary trying to determine our possible options.

Like my children wondering and worrying what they can do to make a good impression on their teachers on the first day of school. Just notice how carefully they select their blouses, socks, and even the ribbons for their hair. Or how they choose their pencil cases and notebooks to impress their friends lest their social status decrease without these efforts.

Worry.

Speak to your family or close friends. Let them unload and reveal their hidden skeletons. Ask them what troubles them most. Invariably at least half the time it will be worrying over something that might happen.

Most of us can cope with our issues — even extremely difficult ones. But few of us can deal with the worry of the vast unknown. The "what might happen if..." creates turmoil within. And even when we are genuinely facing a difficult tribulation, what sends us into the abyss is often worrying about the challenge getting worse. What if the pain gets more severe? What if the stress becomes more intense?

Your mother may be able to cope with the arthritic pain in her joints now, but she can't handle the worry of what might happen ten years down the road when the pain intensifies, as she ages.

Your cousin might be managing on his rainy day savings now that he has suddenly been laid off from his job, but he worries about what will happen when that runs dry.

Your friend who is overweight worries about gaining extra pounds and becoming prone to heart disease or diabetics.

And your colleague might be financially secure now, but worries what if the plunging stock market crashes further and the investments for his future dwindle.

And, of course, your children can usually cope with the demands of their teachers and school friends once the school year begins, but they worry, at its start, about the vast unknown of how it will be.

So, in truth, worry is at least half of the problem. Removing worry from our emotional dictionaries would be curing at least half of our psychological and physical maladies.

Perhaps that is why thinking positively is such an adage in Judaism. Positive thinking creates positivity, first by removing half of the troubling issue — which is our worry — and next by fostering in us a comforting belief of a greater Being, further opening the spiritual channels for recovery.

So the next time you worry about your job, your health, your relationships, your finances, your aging parents, or your children's first day of school, why not stop to reflect: How can I infuse my circumstances with positive energy and positive thinking to create a more positive outcome?

As for the chronic worriers, like myself, here's a new worry: will I ever stop worrying?

୬ *Positive thinking nurtures a belief in G-d and opens the channels for a positive influx of goodness into our lives.*

Soon, Soon!

"When will Sara Leah finally fit into this adorable outfit?"

My thirteen-year old daughter loves to coordinate my newborn's wardrobe. At least once a week, while caressing a particularly cute new outfit, she asks me this question.

"Soon, honey, before you know it!" I answer with what has become my uniform response.

"When will Sara Leah be big enough to..." has become the chorus from my children. They repeat this daily mantra as they eagerly anticipate the time when Sara Leah will *finally* crawl, walk, talk, or be big enough to do a slew of other activities. Ever since the day she was born, they wanted to know when they would no longer have to be so careful to hold up her head, when her little fingers would be able to grab a rattle, when she'd be able to laugh with them.

I often find myself silently joining ranks with my children's restless impatience as I, too, wonder when my newborn will finally sleep through the night, get into a proper schedule, and not need to be rocked incessantly. But as I fall into this pattern of willing her to be older, I try to remember that it will be "too soon, before I know it!"

Being that Sara Leah is my sixth child, I have the wisdom of hindsight and experience to realize just how fast time escapes us.

Not very long ago, I was coming home from the hospital carrying a swaddled beautiful newborn. How similar to Sara Leah that infant appeared, but how quickly she transformed into my seventeen-year-old daughter. I still cannot fathom how close to two decades could have vanished so hastily and craftily.

While expecting Sara Leah, too, I willed the days to go by quicker. Then, several months ago, in the early months of my pregnancy, I was struck by how quickly the cycle of life turns — just as I was sitting at the unexpected funeral of my father-in-law.

Though he was in his early eighties at the time of his passing, my father-in-law's death was sudden. He had been weak for a while, but it felt like just yesterday that he had visited us, robust and healthy, in Toronto.

Gleeful excitement had filled our home then as Zeidy had presented my oldest children with their first bicycles — a bright red one for my son and a pretty pastel-pink one for my daughter. Now, these teenage children were at my side in this large room, despondently accompanying him on his last journey.

While listening to the eulogies, I thought how ironic that I was carrying the gift of life just at the moment when we were lamenting its departure. But, with or without our consent, the rhythm of life hastily dances forward, unabated.

So, as I experience a day that feels like it is just creeping by with endlessly long moments filled with bouts of newborn crying that just can't be placated, I try to discover a perspective. Or, as I pass by the pictures of my children hanging on the walls of my home in the wee hours of the night, with my newborn cradled over my shoulder, I see tangible proof of how quickly children grow up and how rapidly life progresses.

And I try to remind myself how important it is to experience and treasure each and every one of these moments.

∾ *Cherish your time and savor its every moment; it passes far too quickly to will it away.*

Stormy Winds

Here in Toronto we've had a long and arduous winter. In fact, I don't remember the last time we had such a cold, snowy, gloomy stretch.

My youngest son has only the faintest recollection of sun-drenched days spent luxuriating lazily outdoors in the park. He vaguely recalls blowing soap bubbles on our front porch, swimming in his wading pool in our backyard, or riding on his tricycle along the sidewalk in front of our home. As the dark winter days drag on, he innocently wonders whether he will ever again do these things.

His swimming trunks, T-shirts, and shorts nestled in the back of his closet provide the only proof that a different climate ever existed. Occasionally, we open these unused drawers to look at these relics from a distant past.

As the dreary days drag on, my children (like almost every adult I encounter) wonder if winter will ever end.

My eleven-year-old daughter, forever the optimist, earnestly reassures me that she can almost "feel" spring in the air. I nod skeptically as I remind her to button the top button of her coat and tie her scarf.

Surprisingly, however — as if nature hears my daughter's optimistic pleas — the next day a warm front brings a southern breeze, melting piles of snow along the road's edge. The streets fill with smiling faces of passersby, who, like us, shed hats, boots, and gloves to embrace the outdoors. My children and I are energized by this much needed taste of spring, a small ray of hope in an endlessly bleak frigidity.

Sure enough, though, days later comes a blast of cold Arctic air and a heavy, thorough blanketing of snow. Once again, the roads and sidewalks are obscured by complete and utter whiteness. The streets empty as the neighborhood returns to hibernation.

As my children and I stand and gaze dreamily out our living room window, I contemplate our long and icy *galut* (exile). I think about the days of warm interspersions of spring air which sent a new energy pulsating through our veins a decade ago, invigorating us with renewed hope of the dawning of a new era, signaled by the disintegration of the Russian communist regime and the astonishing display of G-d's hand protecting the Land of Israel from thirty-nine Scud missiles during the Gulf War.

But as quickly and unexpectedly as these signs appeared, they have been followed by even more frigid blasts as our hopes of a warmer tomorrow were so helplessly dashed. The Land of Israel is besieged daily by the horrors of suicide bombers wreaking pain and destruction. The tragedy of September 11 hit us hard, and till today terrorism leaves a trail of thousands of broken and devastated families. Today the world scene seems as insecure and troubling as ever.

I stand looking out the window of our history at a horizon of dark desolation as new clouds of war are being forecast daily and uncertainty penetrates our souls.

But as February closes and March turns the corner, I realize that although I get more desperate with each chilling day, I also know with certainty that each passing day draws us one day closer to a better, brighter, and warmer tomorrow.

With my children at my side, I gaze out my living room window to a world of desolate whiteness. I realize that if I try hard enough, my children's ever present faith and optimism can infect my own mood of despair. Outside, the blizzard rages as hard as ever; but when I muster enough effort, I can almost hear the sounds of my children's laughter as they play merrily on a sun-drenched porch, blowing carefree soap bubbles.

And as I do, I envision a new season on the world's horizon, ushering in a brighter future of world peace, harmony, and redemption — now one day closer.

   ❧ *As life's clouds loom pessimistically bleak, remember that the silver lining is just around the corner.*

Bitachon:
Reflections on Trust

She stands.

She falters.

She takes an uncertain step forward.

She falls backward, landing hard. Momentarily confused, she struggles to regain her composure. A soft sob escapes her mouth.

She looks up at me. Waiting for me.

She feels my arms around her. Comforting her. Embracing her with confidence and trust.

She prepares to take a step once again. She has an expression of determination on her face; her eyes are focused with purpose, her lips pursed with resolve.

She flexes her leg muscles. Slowly she raises herself upright, one knee at a time. Soon she is standing. Victoriously.

She is absolutely absorbed in the task at hand. She's not looking up at me anymore. She doesn't need to. She knows I'm there.

She sees me applauding her accomplishment, encouraging her,

prodding her onward. For the moment, she is full of contentment.

How long will it last? When will she stumble again? It doesn't matter. This moment she is happy. She doesn't consider the next fall, or the next. She doesn't need to.

She is confident that she can deal with them.

For she knows I am here for her. She knows I will be here for her. She feels the warmth of my embrace. And she trusts me.

She doesn't think of the times that I allowed her to fall. She doesn't understand why I didn't catch her those times, every time. She doesn't make such calculations. She doesn't think in such terms. She doesn't need to.

Because she trusts me. Wholeheartedly. Implicitly.

She knows beyond any doubt that I won't allow her to get hurt. She knows I will have a warm embrace, a hug and a kiss for her always. She knows there is nothing better than being in my outstretched arms.

She knows that I *am*, and always *will be*, there for her.

She is my ten-month-old baby daughter, learning how to walk.

But *she* is also each and every one of us, learning how to grow.

In speaking of our relationship with You, we sometimes speak of our *bitachon*, "trust." Other times we speak of our *emunah*, our "faith."

Bitachon is the warm embrace that we feel, the assurance that we find in the depths of our heart and soul, that You are watching, caring, and holding us.

It is without calculations.

It is the simple certainty, the assuredness that You are with us.

It is the warm embrace my baby daughter feels when she struggles and stumbles in learning to walk. It is the hug in the wee hours of the night that makes all monsters disappear for my six-year-old son. It is the heart-to-heart talk that solves all friendship problems for my ten-year-old daughter. And it is the knowledge for my teenage son that, at any point in his life, he will have a listening ear and practical help available to him.

ও ঙ

Bitachon differs from *emunah*. The two are almost paradoxical. *Emunah* is the *faith* that all You do is good for us. That You are infinitely wiser than us and understand better than we what we must go through in life to reveal our strengths and actualize our potentials.

Emunah helps us when we look back at the trials of our lives. *Emunah* is how my six-year-old will look back at a punishment for inappropriate behavior, realizing, in retrospect, that his parents have treated him fairly, setting limits to help him develop as a person. *Emunah* is how my daughter will look at an imposed consequence for leaving a messy room, understanding that her parents want to inculcate in her positive personality traits.

Emunah helps us deal with the *past*. To come to terms with the difficulties and failures, the hardships and the blows, that life showers on us. It is the *faith* in knowing it was all for the best. That for some reason beyond our comprehension it *had* to be this way.

But *bitachon* assists us with the *present* and the *future*. It is my uncalculated *trust*, the warmth all around me, right now, at this moment, because You are with me.

It is the confidence that You will provide only good things for me in the future because You are the ultimate source of good. It is jumping from the cliff, while knowing that the landing will be soft, because Your arms will be carrying me. It is the certitude that You will chase away all of life's monsters. That you are there with me in each and every new venture.

While *emunah* confronts the pain of my past falls, *bitachon* is the confidence that enables me to attempt to take that next step forward.

ও *Experience your inner child's bitachon, an absolute trust and confidence that everything will be good.*

These journal questions reflect values from the stories you just heard. Record your answers for a greater awareness of your spiritual perspective on life.

On Positive Thinking
JOURNAL

1. Describe a situation when your positive thinking affected the outcome.

2. Make a list of your worries. Next to each worry write something proactive that you can do to alleviate the worry.

3. Resolve to eliminate those worries that you have no control over.

4. Identify practical ways that you can feel more positive in your day.

5. Describe a situation where you overcame a fear or insecurity. What steps did you take to successfully do so?

6. Identify two of your fears or insecurities.

7. How does your approach to fear affect its outcome?

On Priorities

Sizing Up a Situation

One Sunday morning, at the crack of dawn, my youngest child came jumping into my bed. Laughingly, he poked at my groggy eyes and smothered my cheeks with wet kisses as he tried to entice me to wake up and begin an adventurous day.

At first I didn't even bother to acknowledge his presence, hopeful that he'd return to his own bed. It took several minutes and several grunts on my part before I was ready to give up my early morning snooze. But eventually, as usual, his enthusiastic demeanor was contagious, and he won me over. I succumbed to his pleas and sat up.

Enthusiastically, he skipped off the short distance to his bedroom, returning seconds later with a storybook to read aloud to him. Cuddling under my cozy blanket covers, we perused the book together, examining its colorful pictures and imagining how the plot would unfold.

Before long, the sun rose and began peeking through the large bay windows on the southern wall of my bedroom. Soon the sun was shining brightly, and after a few moments, its brilliant glare blinded us from continuing further.

Undeterred, my son raised his small hands and placed his stubby fingers right in front of his eyes, blocking the sun's powerful rays.

"See," he announced. "My hand blocks the sun."

"Yes," I agreed.

Pensively, he continued, "That's because my hand is much larger than the sun."

To prove his point, he cuddled closer to me and placed his hands before both of our eyes, obscuring from us the sun's glare.

"See," he demonstrated. "My hand blocks the sun's light because it is larger than the sun."

I giggled at his reasoning. "No, honey. The sun is much larger. Your hand is only able to block the sun's rays because you are putting your hands right in front of your eyes, so your eyes no longer see the sun.

"You see," I continued, "things that are closer to you always seem larger than those that are farther away."

We then compared the sizes of different objects in my bedroom. Together we looked at the dresser that seemed so small from afar, but much larger once we placed our hands on it. And though from a distance the bedside lamp, the hanging mirror, and the picture frames appeared smaller than my son's hand, as we approached them we saw how each was really much larger.

For a little while, until it was time to get busy with the chores of the day, we walked around the room placing our hands on each item, noting their sizes from different vantage points.

As the day continued and all sorts of issues and pressures that arise in day-to-day living came up, I tried to apply the lesson that I had taught my youngster that morning.

The closer an object or issue is to you, the less objectivity you have in measuring its correct size or importance. Far too often a problem looms so large, masking its real size or blocking other meaningful issues.

Maybe that lesson was even worth losing my early Sunday morning snooze over.

    ♾ *Take a step back to analyze whether small issues in your life are obscuring the whole picture. Try looking at problems from closer up or farther away so that their real dimensions – and, often, insignificance – surfaces.*

Moon Watching

With an active household and a busy lifestyle, my day, like most people's, is full of many mundane chores that need to be done as part of the routine schedule. One afternoon, after having just completed one such chore and in the rush to head off to begin the next one, I called to my four-year-old son. "Bundle up in your coat. We need to pick up a few things from the grocery store," I instructed as I scribbled a quick shopping list, while my mind composed a mental to-do list to be taken care of once we returned.

Opening the car door for my son, I waited while he climbed in. He pointed to the clear blue sky and observed, "Look, Ma. We can see the moon even though it is daytime."

"Yes, dear," I nodded absentmindedly and motioned for him to get settled in his seat.

During the short drive to the grocery store, my son's gaze was fixated on his window as he continued to watch the celestial skies. When we arrived at our destination several blocks away, my son was still transfixed by the moon.

"Look, Ma." This time he exclaimed in wonder, "The moon keeps following me wherever I go!"

I chuckled as I explained to him, "Actually, honey, the moon *seems* like it is moving and following you wherever you are. Really, it is not moving along with you. It is just so large that even though it is far away, you can see it wherever you are. So it feels like it is accompanying you everywhere."

◈ ◈

As I went with my son up and down the rows of the supermarket aisles, I thought some more about the moon and its presence. I thought about how, sometimes, we get so caught up in the rush of mundane activities and chores that we forget to allow the big things or the "big picture" to accompany us.

At times, we may feel seemingly far away from the big and important issues of life — like the purpose of why we are here and what we are meant to achieve. We get carried away coping with the "small" mundane activities and chores of everyday existence. But, even then, we must not lose sight of the big raison d'être: we need to allow it to accompany and follow us wherever we go, like the moon.

So I slowed down somewhat as I walked up and down those aisles and listened a little more carefully to my son's chatter, realizing that he fit very well into the category of this big picture. And when we exited the store, I took the extra minute, together with my son, to gaze in wonder at how the large moon in the sky was still following us wherever we went.

I've since used up all those groceries that I purchased at the supermarket that afternoon. But I hope I will continue to keep in good supply the bigger discoveries I found in the aisles that afternoon.

❧ In the rush of day-to-day life, don't lose sight of the bigger picture — the reason you are here.

Wiped Out

Visiting my husband's family in Lakewood, New Jersey, is never easy. It means an eleven-hour drive with a car full of children. No simple feat. Add to that the unknown variable of weather conditions in the winter season, and the equation becomes even more complex.

But family is family, and you make the effort.

So when a niece was getting married in the wintertime, we ignored the weather forecast warnings, packed into the van, and hoped for the best.

Experienced at these long-distance trips, I thought we had finally gotten them down to a science and were prepared for almost any situation. Several days in advance we had our mechanic check and refill the car's fluids, test the pressure in the tires, and do an all-around examination for any other possible problems. Having passed his scrutinizing eye, I was certain that our relatively new minivan was fit for the trip.

Next, I had my eldest daughters prepare and pack a slew of car activities. Little knapsacks were stuffed with crayons, small crafts, and activity books, as well as favorite cuddling toys.

And finally, perhaps most importantly, we visited the local supermarket and purchased all the latest varieties of snacks and confections. Seeing the sweets that they would be bribed with for good car behavior, the children's eyes glazed over in anticipation.

Piling into the van, we all got comfortable for the long haul. Surprisingly, the hours passed smoothly. Even the weather held up, and we had almost completely clear conditions throughout our drive.

We arrived without event in good timing at our destination and had a pleasant stay. Bright and early a few mornings later, we brushed off about a foot of snow from our van to set off for our return trip. Within minutes, we noticed that the van's windshield wipers were stuck. Hoping that they were simply frozen, we waited a few more minutes as the car heated, to no avail.

"Maybe it's just a fuse," suggested my husband. Though freezing rain had begun to pour, we drove carefully down the block to the nearest mechanic. "If it's a fuse, he should be able to fix it immediately, and we can be on our way," he assured me, and I smiled with relief.

Moments later, we discovered that it wasn't the fuse after all. The wiper's motor needed a replacement part which, unfortunately, wasn't in stock and would take a day to order.

We contemplated traveling without the wipers, but with the heavy rains now falling, our vision was completely obscured. Driving only one block was all it took for us to make a sharp U-turn and head back.

The incident, while rather minor, made me realize something important. In life, we can be as prepared as possible for any eventuality. We may think that we have made all the necessary arrangements. Equipped for the long haul, we have all the essential components — physical fitness and health, a well-paying job, close friends and contacts. We may even have driven a fair distance, successfully realizing many of our goals.

But without a perspective and a strong sense of identity, all of these provisions become utterly useless. Along comes a storm, and suddenly you realize that you are stuck to your spot. Without an unobstructed view (or at least a small cleared area on your windshield) of what's really important in life and how to proceed, you become immobile, despite the comprehensive preparations.

Life has its ways of showering all kinds of storms upon us. Rarely do the horizons remain completely clear, regardless of what precautions we may have taken.

Perhaps these downpours are meant to remind us just how vital a clear vision is for journeying forward.

> ❧ *Clear your vision by composing a mental list of what is important and valuable to you. Survive life's rainstorms by reminding yourself of your real priorities.*

Unknown Variables

I t's been a while since I practiced tenth-grade mathematics, but the other night, when my daughter came over to me looking rather dejected, I thought I would give it a try.

Always a whiz at her schoolwork, this time she was having difficulty and needed some assistance.

Every problem in her assigned exercise was composed of two equations, each with two unknown variables labeled "x" and "y." The instructions read: (1) Communicate the relationship between each of the unknown numbers. (2) Isolate the x or the y. (3) Determine the values of each of the unknowns to solve the equation.

My daughter had spent time working on these problems only to come up with incorrect answers. She had tried and tried, and at this point her forehead was knotted in deep concentration and frustration.

Mathematics had never been one of my favorite subjects, so I wasn't very confident that I could help. But when a child comes to you looking and feeling so discouraged, you put aside your insecurities, roll up your sleeves, and get to work, albeit somewhat hesitantly.

We began tackling the first problem. Fortunately, my memory

jogged. It was like getting onto a bicycle after not riding for years. At first you feel a little wobbly and uncertain, but then the skill kicks in and you're riding confidently.

One at a time, we worked through each equation. On closer observation, I could see that my daughter generally understood the necessary skills. Most of her errors had actually been quite minor, merely careless computation.

Once she saw where she had gone off track, my daughter gained the self-assurance to proceed independently, and before long, the task was completed. The previous lines of tension on her face were replaced with a radiant smile, expressing relief and gratitude.

Working on those math problems sharpened more than just my math skills. I discovered some essential yet basic principles that can be applied to life.

Life is full of equations. We confront a new set of equations at every change in our circumstances, at every new stage of our maturation. Each equation communicates to us what our relationship is with ourselves, our world, and other people.

But every stage of life has unknowns. Our challenge is to figure out these unknown variables, so that we can find the solutions that make our lives correct and true.

Here are the lessons I learned from my daughter's math exercise:

1. Tackle only one problem at a time. Otherwise the load becomes too great to bear and you risk capitulating out of frustration or defeat.

2. Isolate the problem or the unknown, and you will have taken the first step on the road to your solution. Otherwise, if you combine all the unknowns, the equation becomes impossible to solve.

3. Finally, we all make miscalculations. Realize the difficulty in finding the flaws in your own work. It may

take the eye of experience or wisdom or objectivity to determine where you are making a mistake.

The exercise concluded, my daughter wanted to know if I, in my school years, had gotten straight A's in math.

Now that's a variable I intend to leave unknown – and unsolved.

୭ *Take problems one step at a time and be big enough to seek help in figuring out where you err.*

Big or Little?

"When someone becomes bigger," four-year-old Yisroel observed one night as I was snuggling with him at bedtime, "their cheeks stop being so chubby."

"Yes, that is true," I affirmed, gently patting his dimpled cheek. "At what point does someone become 'bigger'?" I queried.

"Well," he contemplated thoughtfully, "at every birthday, a person becomes bigger and bigger." He demonstrated with his arms an imaginary person growing larger and larger as he spoke.

"And at which birthday does someone switch from being considered 'little' to 'big'?" I probed.

Without a moment's hesitation, he replied, "Someone who is three years old is little, but once he turns four, he becomes big."

"How about when someone turns five?" I suggested, since he was eagerly anticipating his fifth birthday, still a few months away. "Will you still think that four was big?"

"For sure," he rejoined confidently.

"How about when you are eight years old, will you *still* think of four as a big age?" I particularly chose the number eight, being the age of his older sister whom he greatly admired. In his perception, she was *really* big since she was able to tie her own shoelaces and ride on a two-wheeler without training wheels.

Without missing a beat, he replied, "Yup."

"And will you still think four is big when you become *sixteen*?" I emphasized the last word, mentioning the age of his oldest sibling and occasional babysitter.

The emphatic nod of his head indicated a resounding yes.

Changing tactics, I suggested, "Do you remember when you had your third birthday?" When he nodded in the affirmative, I continued, "When you stopped being two years old, did you think then that being three was big?"

He pondered a moment before replying, slightly impatiently, "No, Mommy. Three years old *is* little. But four years, now that is a-l-w-a-y-s big!"

∾ ∾

Our bedtime discussion accentuated to me the difficulty in seeing beyond the point where we are at in life. Yisroel's little mind couldn't fathom ever considering four years old as anything but "big" because that was how he saw it now; and in his mind, he would forever see it as such.

Like small children, we, too, are often unable to contemplate beyond the here and now. We are unable to fathom that our opinions or decisions might be anything other than the only or best way to proceed. Despite knowing that over time and with a broadened perspective, our opinions might change dramatically, we nevertheless confidently and stubbornly assert our preconceived stances.

We need to be "big" enough in life to incorporate other voices of wisdom and experience to enhance our own narrow stances.

∾ ∾

I kissed Yisroel good night. As I tiptoed from his room, I whispered tenderly, "Good night, my big boy."

A proud smile broke across his chubby cheeks as he replied, "Goodnight, my big Mommy."

    ❧ Don't allow your own perspective to remain forever stationary. Allow it to grow and develop by opening your mind to options outside your limited framework.

Morning Routines

Flab!

It's the dreaded word.

Anyone who has passed the age of thirty (or any woman who has given birth to more than one child) has, at one point in her life, come face to face with it. Beads of sweat form along your brow as you realize that it has you ensnared in its loathsome clutches.

In a society where our quest for health, longevity, and youthfulness reigns supreme, fatty flab must be avoided at all costs. Advertisements besiege us with the glamor of a slender body and the health benefits and extra energy perks of being physically fit.

So I decided, one ambitious day, to take this fitness ideal by its reins. I was determined to control any unwanted inches.

From the back crevice of my closet, out came my dusty sneakers as I vowed to maintain a weekly routine. Outfitted in comfortable clothes with my favorite, fast-paced tape cassette in hand, I headed off to my corner room and dusted off my exercise machines, which had been retrieved from a neighbor's garage sale a couple of years ago, also in a moment of ambitious idealism.

I turned on the answering machine so I wouldn't be interrupted by any phone calls, and I warned my children in my best no-nonsense voice, "Mommy is busy." They could join me if they like, but under no circumstances could they disturb. I was finally prepared to take the plunge.

In my first exercise routine, my joints creaked under the strain, but I stubbornly pushed forward. Strenuously, I counted the sets of sit-ups and leg pushes and timed the minutes on the machines until I had reached my goals, little by little, moment by moment, one push-up at a time.

Sweaty but satisfied, my first session was successfully over. Physically I was a little sore, but at the same time revitalized and re-plete with energy to tackle any challenge that came my way. I real-ized then that this would have to become a part of my regular morning routine. I would have to find the few extra minutes each day.

That was when it struck me that, just as a physical routine is important for maintaining our health, the same rules for success ap-ply to a spiritual routine. Becoming fit and unflabby spiritually means carving out the daily moments from your hectic lifestyle for a spiritual suffusion. It means energizing your day by starting off your morning permeated with words of Torah inspiration.

Is it difficult to find the time? Is it a strain on your concentra-tion? Does the phone beckon? Are the kids tugging? Are work obliga-tions summoning you? Or do the million and one other things in your hectic twenty-first-century lifestyle pull you in different direc-tions?

Take charge. Set the tone. Find a comfortable place, and deter-mine a realistic pace.

Don't expect immediate results, just as the mirror won't bear wit-ness to your first exercise attempts. But begin a little at a time, a few minutes a day, one day at a time. Build up your resistance, increase your level of strength, develop your mind's agility, and, voila, before you know it, you'll be spiritually energized all week long.

After all, we all hate flab — physical or spiritual.

Now, if I can only make sure to continue this exercise routine through my second day...

  ❧ *Carve out daily moments to connect to your true inner calling and your spirituality.*

Celebrating Each Moment

Today marks the first day of school. Today, all of my children return to a regular schedule of formal learning after weeks and weeks of being the masters of their own time, much of which was spent in and around our home. I wave goodbye as my last and youngest child rushes from the front porch to his waiting car pool and gently close the front door.

I admit that I eagerly anticipated this moment. The weeks of unstructured vacation, while immensely enjoyable, were also hectic. Juggling my own schedule of work and obligations with the children's natural desires for nonstop outings, recreational activities, and endless activities was challenging.

Don't get me wrong. I love to be surrounded by my children and to while away the time relaxing in their company. But still, almost guiltily, I eagerly anticipated some quiet moments. Just the thought of lingering over my morning hot mug of coffee in absolute serenity sent waves of delicious pleasure through my mind.

As I close the front door and turn toward my kitchen, I note that there are no longer toys strewn across the living room floor for me to trip over. As I place the broom back in the closet, I think how today it would stay there, unlike the many recent days when it would be put to good use several times within an hour.

Polishing the kitchen table and quickly rinsing the remaining breakfast dishes, I know that my counters will remain gleaming all day, free of smudges from dirty little fingerprints.

Returning the milk to its place in the refrigerator, I know that today I won't need to incessantly remind my youngsters to close the fridge door after each of their many visits investigating its contents.

There will be no shoes, sweaters, or socks to pick up from the floor. No wooden building blocks or toy cars to put away. No spills to wipe. No remnants of craft paper to gather. No muddy footprints to scrape off the floor.

There will be no perpetual chatter, no complaints of boredom, and no heated arguments requiring a referee.

Silence reigns. Utter silence.

Luxuriating over my second mug of coffee in the stillness of the moment, I can hear a lone bird chirping outdoors as I watch the silver clouds dance elegantly across the vast sky.

Peaceful tranquility.

Only the subtly creaking floor and the distant sound of the laundry machine whirring in the background breaks the silence.

And then, suddenly, without explanation, the peaceful quiet that I enjoyed but a moment earlier turns eerie. The stillness becomes oppressive, haunting with its deafening silence. Suddenly, inexplicably, I long for the peals of laughter, for the pulls of little hands on my skirt. I miss the hugs, the ceaseless inquisitive questions, and the round cheeks smothered with chocolate to plant kisses on.

My serene home has become a place of lonely walls and rooms. The moment of calm, anticipated for weeks, has metamorphosed into an oppressive emptiness.

❧ ❧

Though it was my children who began school on that September morning, I learned an invaluable lesson. Sometimes we impatiently await an upcoming event. It may be a new stage of a child's growth or development or a new change in our circumstances. In your anticipation, however, do not overlook the present. Savor each moment, each current phase — its cheerful parts together with its nuisances. Moments pass far too quickly not to celebrate each one fully.

Moreover, even the best of moments, experienced alone, become meaningless. Real joy is only in those special times shared with another.

When my children return home a few hours later on that same day, I look a little more affectionately at the smudges of chocolate on my counters and the muddy footprints on my floors.

   The celebration of life is in relishing each of its moments — especially those shared with others.

A Lesson on Love

Three-year-old Yisroel was closest in age to his older sister, Shira. So it was natural that he felt the greatest affinity toward her, learned from her, and loved to mimic just about everything she did. Shira was his natural playmate and therefore was also the one with whom, on occasion, he fought the most.

When Shira went to stay over at a classmate's home one day, Yisroel was devastated. Throughout the day he paced the toy room and wondered aloud how long it would be until Shira's return. Several times he complained about how lonely, bored, and upset he was feeling without her.

"Mommy, when is Shira finally coming home?" Yisroel whined for the fifth time that hour. "Why did you let her go away for s-u-c-h a long, long time?" In his inimitable three-year-old style, he asked over and over. After all, to him a whole day was an eternity.

"Yisroel, I can see how much you are missing Shira," I empathized. "But, why is it that when Shira is at home, you sometimes fight with her and you don't play so nicely?" I questioned gently, hoping to at least develop this into a learning experience for him.

"Mommy, you see, it's like this." Yisroel paused from his activity, and his facial expressions suddenly became thoughtful and mature.

"I love Shira very much, so I miss her when she is gone. But sometimes, when I am playing with her, I fight."

Staring me squarely in the eye, he continued simply, "That's because I forget just how much I love her!"

> ❧ *Those whom we love and interact with the most, we often argue or disagree with the most. A pause can make us reflect how meaningful the other is to us.*

Driving Rules for Life's Roadways

"Next year at this time, I'll be able to drive myself," my fifteen-year-old daughter reminded me for the third time that week as I drove her to a friend's home one evening.

I vividly remember my own enthusiasm two decades ago when I, too, was her age awaiting this newfound freedom. Having just moved to a suburb of Toronto far away from friends and school, my parents encouraged me to drive. My old jalopy became the envy of my friends as I experienced the autonomy as well as the responsibility that driving a car entails.

I also remember how, years later, before leaving my parents' home to establish my own, I encouraged my own mother, in a later stage of her life, to learn this vital skill. I was gratified, for once, to reverse roles and reciprocate a tiny part of the support and patience that I had learned from her. To this day she expresses her gratitude for my perseverance.

So, as my oldest daughter prepared to get behind the wheel of the driver's seat and face this new stage of her life, I couldn't help but reminisce how just yesterday I cautiously bundled her into the infant car seat as my husband drove us home from the hospital where she was born.

Lying in her infant seat then, she was a passive observer, accommodated and catered to by those around her. Now she has developed into an active participant, prepared to give and do for others. She is ready to contribute to her environment.

Then, she was in the back seat, enjoying the ride. Now, she is ready to take on the challenge of the driver's reins.

At this monumental juncture in her life, I try to think of what insight I can provide her as she confronts these new challenges. She will learn many of the dos and don'ts of driving from her instructors. But here are the life lessons that I will try to impress upon her as she encounters her new roadways:

1. In your haste to get to your destination, don't drive too fast. Aside from missing the beauty of the surrounding scenery, you will speed past important road signs providing direction and guidance.

2. On the other hand, don't drive so slowly that you become sidetracked and forget your destination — and goal — altogether.

3. Realize that you are not the only one on your journey. Leave room and have consideration for those sharing the road.

4. Carelessness, even momentarily, can cause untold damage to yourself and those around you.

5. Despite your most vigilant efforts, remember that there are still blind spots in your field of vision. Realize this so that you can make the necessary allowances.

6. And finally, no matter how extensively you study

the rules of driving, nothing equals the real test of experience on the road.

৯ *In life, like in driving, proceed with caution, never losing focus of your goals and priorities.*

These journal questions reflect values from the stories you just heard. Record your answers for a greater awareness of your spiritual perspective on life.

On Priorities
JOURNAL

1. Describe a situation in your life when something small gained too much significance.

2. Identify three real priorities in your life.

3. At the end of the day, write down two things you did that were significant.

4. Give an example of how a narrow perspective led you to a wrong conclusion.

5. What do you believe is your personal calling – the reason you are here?

6. How have you carved out time today to be in touch with your spirituality and your inner calling?

On the Power of Deed

My Children's Prayers

Esther had just replaced the telephone receiver when Naomi, taking her turn, quickly began dialing. News had just reached us of yet another suicide bombing in Israel, killing, maiming, and wounding dozens more of our brethren.

The students in each of my children's respective grades had decided to join in a united effort of prayer. Each student was asked to call five friends, requesting that they make a chain call to an additional five people, urging them to pray for those hurt in the attack.

Esther, having completed her calls, sat down with a book of *Tehillim* (Psalms) on her lap, ready to begin. Naomi would, momentarily, follow suit.

Meanwhile, seven-year-old Shira was observing her older sisters closely. An intelligent girl, she understood the severity of what had occurred. With an intent look on her face, Shira was searching for a way that she, too, could somehow contribute.

A moment later, my determined youngest daughter had her three-year-old brother's plump hand in hers as she led him to the living room couch. She made sure they were both comfortably seated before opening up her own book of *Tehillim*.

Shira searched for the shortest two chapters in the book. Then, with great care and effort, she began to recite each word in her most authoritative voice, waiting patiently for her brother to repeat after her. The two continued in this manner, word by word and verse by verse.

The vowels of several of these unfamiliar words were muddled in Shira's pronunciation and became even less intelligible once Yisroel was through with his repetition. Nevertheless, the two joyously prodded on, slowly and steadily, until two whole chapters had been recited.

Occasionally, Shira paused to comment, "Good job, Yisroel!" This, as well as Shira's most no-nonsense voice, kept Yisroel rapt until they successfully had completed Shira's self-appointed task.

A few moments later, Shira triumphantly turned to her younger brother and in a sweet voice asked, "Do you know why we just said that?" Once again, she was assuming the role of teacher.

Yisroel's blue eyes widened, and he gave her his full attention.

"Because," she continued, "many people keep getting hurt in Israel. We are praying for them. And now, since we both asked so nicely, Hashem (G-d) will listen to our prayers and make sure that no more Jews get hurt." She smiled at her brother confidently.

"Yes." Hanging onto her every word and smiling in return, Yisroel parroted, "Now Hashem will listen, and no more Jews will get hurt."

Shira then closed her book, and hand in hand the two skipped over to return it to its proper place on the bookshelf. Both were smiling from ear to ear, satisfied with their accomplishment and without a shred of doubt in their minds that G-d would follow their complete bidding.

At many difficult junctures in my own life, I have reflected on the attitude of my young children. I marvel at their childlike confidence that everything will be good. I envy their unshakable trust in G-d, that He has heard their requests and will respond immediately and positively.

And I deeply admire their complete certainty that their personal contributions will make a difference, convinced that each of their prayers is valuable and urgently needed.

If more of us would foster our own inner child's perception of reality — not one of arrogance, but rather of confidence, that each of our actions count — I believe each of us would be trying that much harder and accomplishing that much more.

And perhaps G-d would then listen to us — even more often.

᠙ *Tap into your inner child's perception that your every small deed is invaluable.*

Monster Dreams

"Mommy! Mommy!" Sobbing loudly, Naomi ran into my bedroom in the middle of the night for the fourth time that week. A recurring nightmare kept waking her from her sleep.

"Was it the same dream?" I inquired, knowing what her answer would be as I rubbed the remnants of sleep from my weary eyes.

Her nod and the terrified expression on her features told me more than any words could express. I had heard all the details of the dream, retold several times already. It was a typical child's nightmare, almost identical at each occasion. A bad monster of a man, masked entirely in black, entered our house, walked into her bedroom, and asked her to come with him. When she refused, he began chasing after her. With her heart thumping wildly, she ran faster and faster until she stumbled and fell. He approached her and reached out to grab her, just as she awakened, screaming frantically.

For the next few days, my husband, Isser, and I had tried to reason with our then six-year-old daughter about her dreams. We tried everything. Isser quoted the words of the Sages proving that dreams are meaningless. He told her how sometimes we notice images or events during the day and the mind mixes them together to conjure nightmares that make no sense when we are asleep. He explained how dreams really have no power over us and are nothing to fear.

On and on we both droned, but the disbelieving look in Naomi's frightened green eyes attested that we weren't quite reaching her.

Next, we suggested that she say extra parts of the prayers, with especial care, before going to bed. But in truth, Naomi, a serious and sensitive child by nature, always took her prayers seriously and, almost always read each word carefully while pointing in the siddur (prayer book).

Before bedtime, we also tried showing Naomi how the front doors of our home were locked and how the windows of her bedroom, high up on the second floor, were impenetrable. She nodded, eyes staring widely, but didn't really seem convinced with the logic that a "monster man" would need to enter through such means.

Finally, in desperation, I suggested that Naomi discuss this problem with my father. "Perhaps Sabba will have an idea of what to do," I said hopefully.

Though a busy rabbi with the communal burdens of the entire city on his shoulders, my father, Rabbi Dovid Schochet, patiently lifted Naomi onto his lap and gave her his full attention as though her problem were his most pressing, indeed his only one.

"And tell me what the bad man looked like," he prodded.

Naomi described the grotesque features and the menacing expression. My father questioned her further and attentively listened to her elaborate on all the specific details.

Finally he looked at her very seriously. They both sat in pensive silence for several moments before he continued, "Naomi, do you want me to explain your dream?"

She nodded affirmatively.

"The bad man," my father began, "is the *yetzer hara*, the evil inclination that we all have inside ourselves. He is very bad and ugly and tries to tempt us to follow his evil ways. That's why he asked you to follow him. But you are brave and strong; you refuse. So he tries harder and chases after you. Sometimes he even makes you stumble and fail or do something wrong, like not acting nicely to your siblings or friends or not following your parents or teacher's instructions." He paused for a moment before continuing, "What do you think you can learn from your dream?"

Naomi's voice faltered for a moment before she confidently replied, "That I must be very strong and not to let his bad hands grab hold of me or convince me to do something wrong."

My father then asked Naomi to suggest practical examples where she could implement this lesson. For the next several minutes, granddaughter and grandfather sat, exploring areas in my daughter's life where there was room for improvement. Eventually the conversation turned more animated, and the laughter of both could be heard.

Since that day, I have thought of my father's approach in confronting my daughter's problem as a road tool for solving life's issues in general.

We all have an inner child within us who is full of fears, insecurities, and vulnerabilities. Validate that inner child's fears; don't discredit them. In order to solve a problem, first you must face it. Only once you look the "monster" squarely in the eye can you hope to transform it. Ignore the monster as meaningless and you haven't solved the problem; you've escaped from it. On the other hand, if you confront the issue, then you are ready to learn how to deal with it.

Furthermore, teach a child, and your own inner child, how to deal with problems on his or her own level, using practical examples. Make the lessons real and relevant by applying it to circumstances in his or her life.

Naomi will still occasionally awaken with this or another recurring nightmare. But these dreams are not coming with nearly as much frequency or intensity anymore. Moreover, the dreams no longer have the same power or devastating effect on her, since now she feels empowered to listen to their message.

　ᔖ *Face your insecurities head on, and you will learn to exploit them as a tool for growth.*

Gestures — Big and Small

The Jewish month of Tishrei is probably one of my favorites. Of course, that has to do with the month brimming over with the whole gamut of holidays ranging from inspirational and cleansing to family-oriented, cheerful, and fun-filled.

But, on a personal note, the twenty-eighth day of this month also marks, for me, a very special life-altering day — my own wedding anniversary.

So this year, as Rosh HaShanah was approaching, I was thinking about anniversaries: the anniversary celebration of when mankind entered into a relationship with You, G-d, as well as my own seventeen-year marriage anniversary.

While seventeen years may sound insignificant, to me it marks the door that opened a whole new world and life.

It feels like yesterday, when, as two youngsters, my husband and I felt such a connection to one another. Though we had our differences, our connection was real nonetheless. And deep. Never could I have imagined at that time that the magnetic bond pulling us together would grow stronger.

But the bond did grow. And almost like elastic, as it tightened around us, it also grew more flexible, providing more room for our respective, independent means of expression.

The differences we had, which hitherto had seemed irreconcilable at times, now seem almost petty. What had before infuriated me — all right, it still upsets me, but now the edge of anger is not as evident. Sometimes, on those rare moments, I even have a glimpse of appreciation for how those differences enhance our connection.

Of course, it also makes all his actions that much more consequential.

I guess with the familiarity we also both let our guard down more. Careless words stumble out more freely. We don't think as much before acting. The small, sweet gestures we did for one another may have become less frequent.

But now his every small effort to please me becomes all the more precious. When he does put that special card on my desk, it means all the more to me.

As I was musing about my upcoming anniversary, the thought struck me. Could it be that this same dynamic is mirrored in our relationship as a nation with You, G-d? True, nowadays we may be spiritually more insensitive to Your wants and wishes than we had been in the past. With our guard down, our deeds may no longer reflect the same nuances of care of previous generations. Our speech and actions don't have the proper consideration and forethought that they are meant to have. We aren't in tune with Your desires as we had been in better times of our national history.

And You, too, don't reveal Yourself as openly as you had to our nation in times gone by. The miracles don't abound. The intimate connection isn't present. Our matrimonial homeland is not imbued with the same holiness and warmth.

But maybe, despite this seeming rift and deficiency in our relationship, the bonds of connection in a way are stronger and superior. Each of our actions counts more and, when it really boils down to it, we're ready to make sacrifices of our very selves for You.

I was caught up in these reflections in the week before Tishrei as I busily went about preparing spiritually and materially for the upcoming holidays. There was so much to do. Meals to cook, soufflés to bake, dresses to purchase, and all the usual hubbub of frenzied household activity for the holiday arrangements.

Then, Wednesday morning, in the midst of these preparations, my husband commented that he must have caught a bad stomach virus. The following morning, a day before the eve of Rosh HaShanah, the bags under his tired eyes revealed that his abdominal pain had not relented but rather had kept him up most of the night. By midday the pain intensified unbearably and was now situated just to the left of his stomach.

A short and immediate visit to the doctor confirmed our worst suspicion. "Rush immediately to the hospital for possible emergency appendix surgery," hastily warned our family physician.

Upon our arrival at the hospital — ignoring the traffic lights, at my husband's urging — I could see that he was doubled over in pain. His ashen face was creased in anxiety.

Seeing him in such inordinate pain, still uncertain of its cause as we waited the endless wait in the hospital emergency room made me feel utterly helpless. Of course, forgotten at this moment was all the holiday preparations. The recipes sitting on my counter for the fancy desserts to be baked or the pants desperately needing hemming were completely disregarded. These and more details were now utterly inconsequential.

Forgotten as well was any and every time in the past that my husband had made a comment that was stupid or reckless. Overlooked were all the times he forgot to take out the garbage or left his jacket thrown over the living room couch, knowing full well how it irked me. Nor did I think of the times he thoughtlessly forgot to express gratitude for the countless things I did for him. The toothpaste tube that he so often carelessly left open didn't enter my mind.

These didn't matter. Not in the slightest. Not now.

As I sat at his bedside, awaiting emergency appendix surgery at 3 a.m. on the eve of Rosh HaShanah, exactly twenty-nine days before our seventeenth anniversary, my thoughts were focused entirely on what I could do to ease his pain.

As I waited in the nearby waiting room while he was wheeled into the operating room, I was only capable of summoning the strength to mouth nonstop prayers begging G-d that no complications arise and that the operation be successful.

And rushing to the recovery room at 4 a.m. on tired feet that had not let up for twenty-two hours as he was groggily wheeled from the successful operation, I could only wish that his recuperation be speedy.

And as he demanded that the doctor release him the following afternoon, just hours before Rosh HaShanah, all I could think of as I drove us home was how to make him more comfortable.

So have the differences between us gone away? Have I learned not to care when he acts inconsiderately or when he forgets the garbage? No, I still care and will care about these things. But what has surfaced over the last seventeen years is a deeper aspect of the relationship than these gestures will ever represent.

Sure, the gestures are nice. And sure we should work on keeping them intact, and even growing. But now, more importantly, was surfacing the bond that had grown and that will hopefully continue to grow. And this bond that was being revealed is far more potent than any gesture possibly could be.

So as I stood in shul on Rosh HaShanah listening to the sound of the shofar, I resolved to make sure to work on those "gestures" that I know are so dear and important to You. This year, I will work on my prayers, on saying my blessings with more concentration, and learn more Torah. I will work as well on my patience and tolerance for those around me and on being more careful with the words that exit from my mouth.

But though I will work on these things, I realize, too, that my personal bond to You, and our collective bond to You as a nation, runs deeper than any of these things possibly could. Our bond to You as a nation means that when it comes right down to it, we are willing to forego our very selves for Your sake.

And standing in shul on Rosh HaShanah, twenty-eight days before my own anniversary, as I resolve to make these improvements for the coming year, I also make one more small resolution.

This year, I will make sure that I buy him an anniversary card — on time.

᪥ *Confronting a difficult situation awakens the profound bond of our special relationships. At such moments, realize the power of each of your small gestures.*

A Letter to
My Eldest Daughter

My dear Esther,

I hope you are enjoying your summer. Though our home is still noisily busy, it feels so lonely and bereft with you so far away. I pass by your empty bedroom and eagerly await your return.

Even your little brother is counting the days. (No doubt, he remembers the small presents you've promised to bring him back!)

But the summer is vanishing so swiftly, and before long we'll be standing at the same airport where we stood waving goodbye to you at the departing gate just weeks ago — but this time, for your enthusiastically anticipated arrival.

I must tell you that I felt so proud when I put down the phone receiver after speaking to you last time. How is it that you have grown so quickly? Can sixteen years have passed in such a flash?!

In my mind's eye, I picture you and your friends as great counselors for your campers. I see the tender sensitivity that you show to your siblings easily transferred to the youngsters in your charge. I can just imagine your creativity, put to such good use, in concocting all kinds of activities, games, and drama programs.

I easily picture, too, your enthusiasm in inspiring your campers with the values of Torah through your warmth and sincerity. It must be a real treat for your campers, some so estranged from this way of life, to have an opportunity to learn so much in such a fun-filled environment of a summer camp.

But what I especially feel pride over is the scene you described over the phone the last time we spoke. You and your fellow counselors were given the opportunity to organize and lead a Shabbaton for the mothers of your campers. You were joined by other women from outlying communities, some who may have never tasted the spirit of an authentic Shabbat.

I easily envision you sitting around a large dining room table laden with Shabbat delicacies. I see you and your friends so articulately explaining the weekly parashah (Torah reading) and sharing interesting stories with the participants — women who are two, three, or even four times your age!

I picture them joining you in spirited song, nodding in agreement at the lessons you convey, and listening intently, mesmerized by the stories you share of the heroism of your grandparents and great-grandparents and our teachers.

But more than the words you communicate, I can hear them listening to your message — the message of you and your friends, girls in their tender teens, speaking with such a sense a purpose, such a deep passion and pride about their heritage and history.

I am not sure if you realize this, but the power of your talks is greater than the articulation of your erudite words. More important than the deepest thoughts that you can brilliantly muster and even more crucial than the excited enthusiasm in your voice is a deeper gift that you have given them.

What you have imparted to these women (as well as to the children in your care) is the essence of what you are, the inner core of what you represent.

And it is this message — a message that is brought home so much more powerfully by a girl your age than by any eloquent adult — that will leave them with such a powerful, lasting impression. Long after you have returned to Toronto, and long after they have forgotten the contents of your speech or the episodes in your stories, the conviction of your words, and the sincerity of your message will linger.

And knowing that you have planted such potent seeds in their hearts with your youthful and vibrant passion makes me burst with pride — just as I wonder how in the world my little girl has grown up so quickly...

Looking forward to seeing you soon and wishing you a safe flight home,

Love always,

Mommy

P.S. Make sure you take some snacks along on the plane — it's a long flight home...

❧ *More important than the words you choose to say is conveying your belief and passion in your sense of purpose.*

Awakenings

It's 3:08 a.m.

UGH.

No, it's not the alarm clock buzzing; it's the baby crying.

I pry open my eyelids, eyes that are heavy like lead, eyes that have been forced to awaken far too few hours ago. I force myself into an upright position. One foot in front of the other. Right foot. Left foot. Right again. Lift the baby...cuddle her...feed her...rock her back to sleep...gently put her back into her crib. Ah, sink back into my own mattress, at last.

It's just one of the routine nighttime feedings that has taken place a few times each night for the last many weeks and months.

These round-the-clock feedings, and having an infant in my home, has reminded me, over and over again, that I am not a master over my time. As much as I try to schedule my day, sure enough the plans are disrupted as my baby clearly brings home the point that time is not in my control.

Nor is it only the constant night feedings or the almost nonexistence of scheduled plans. It's also the constant change that I witness taking place before my eyes — each of her milestones and growths — which proves to me so palpably how time is quickly passing.

With a baby, every week is another birthday. Every day brings a new development. Her first smile. Her first laugh. Her growing alertness. Her outgrowing her first clothes. Her lifting her head and then rolling over. All of these are my baby's constant small reminders to me that time is passing by — swiftly — and that I have no control over its reins.

A poll that I came across recently asked new parents if having a child awakened their spiritual side. A whopping 86 percent responded that since having a baby, they have become more involved in spiritual and religious practices or feel a stronger personal connection to G-d or a Higher Power. Only 3 percent did not feel it was important that their child believe in G-d or a Higher Force.

And though babies have such a pronounced effect on their parents, I don't think their influence is limited to just their parents. I've noticed how the sternest-faced stranger will stop me in the street to return a smile to my baby.

I've seen my younger children, too, come home with sad or angry dispositions. They'll be cross with each other; they'll be unfriendly to me and might even slam a few doors in their sullen moods. But put them alone in the room with the baby, and I'll soon observe gentle cuddles, full smiles, soft tones of voice, and playful tickles as they try to make the baby laugh.

Why the transformation in my children or in apathetic strangers?

I believe babies awaken the softer and more spiritual side in all of us. Seeing a living, breathing baby can soften the hardest, most cynical heart as she bears witness to the awesome miracle of a tiny, but perfect, new life.

But it's more. There's the baby's absolute vulnerability — her needing you and relying on you for everything.

For a parent, this reliance makes you feel a sense of responsibility, not only in caring for her physical needs, but her spiritual ones as well. She beckons you to look deeper, to probe further and to search for answers to the greater meaning and purpose of why we are all here — if not for your own sake, then at least for her sake, to provide her with direction and guidance.

A baby's vulnerability also makes us feel vulnerable and protective. My youngest son, as boys do, will tease his older sisters, play pranks, and rough-and-tumble them. But he'll reserve his softest, gentlest tones for the baby. Her vulnerability and tiny little body makes him so protective of her that woe to any one of his friends who will so much as raise his voice to "his" baby.

Lately my son has also been asking questions about how we all treated him when he was younger. Did he cry a lot? Did we cuddle him and rock him so much? Did he like to play with these same rattles? In his mind's eye, the baby reminds him of a time when he, too, was completely in need of our total help and support.

On his own level, I think my son appreciates what I and so many other parents with a new baby have come to conclude. Just as our little baby is not capable of taking care of herself and her needs, in life each of us is not a master of his or her own destiny and fate. Subconsciously our own vulnerability is awakened as it dawns on us that we are all in the hands of a Force far greater than we.

And finally, I think the constant change taking place in a baby's life opens us up to the realization that we aren't — or shouldn't be — stagnant, static individuals. We are here for a purpose. Our lives have meaning. What we are contributing to our world becomes more pressing as we are constantly made aware, by this rapidly developing child, how time is moving forward.

Each moment, each day, each week, and each month provides us with ample opportunity to reach new milestones, new goals, and new contributions to our environment.

Tucking my baby in after one more night feeding and observing just how much she's grown, I ask myself, how have I?

✤ *Time moves far too quickly not to utilize each passing moment to do, accomplish, and grow.*

Pushing Buttons

Men love toys and gadgets. So it was no surprise to me when my husband returned home one day with the latest gadget. In his hand he held a small black apparatus and was eager to demonstrate its efficacy. He claimed it was vital for the enhancement of the quality of our life.

The new device meant to improve and simplify our morning routine was an automatic car starter.

"Just push here, and, voila, the van will automatically start up," he explained as he pushed one of the small protruding buttons. "If you are indoors, or far from where the van is parked, lift this antenna," he instructed, extending a long silver antenna. "Several minutes before you are ready to head out, press the button, and the van will be all warmed up for you," he concluded with a tone of satisfaction.

Never an enthusiast for electronic gadgets, I listened halfheartedly to his instructions, nodding absentmindedly as he indicated the various buttons for locking, unlocking, and alarming the van.

But the next time that I had occasion to use the automatic starter, I regretted that I hadn't paid closer attention. I pushed the wrong button, and the alarm was triggered. The van started to beep continuously and noisily. Frantically I pressed every button as neighbors and pedestrians disdainfully looked on. By the time my four-year-old son showed me the correct button to press, I was ready to toss out the little wonder machine.

Eventually I did get the hang of the automatic starter. In time, I even enjoyed using it. On icy winter mornings, I appreciated its convenience immensely. Each time, I marveled anew at how the simple pressing of the right button produced such a comfortably warm vehicle.

And then it struck me that we, too, all have automatic starters. Each morning we wake up and have a panoramic choice of buttons to press.

Starting our day with the right frame of mind, in gratitude to our Creator, expressed through our prayers and Torah studies, can get our morning started off on the right track. Pushing the right buttons throughout the day – a nod of encouragement or a welcoming smile to a child, spouse, or acquaintance – can warm you and those around you.

On the other hand, push the wrong button – start off with a negative frame of mind, a harsh word, or a scowling demeanor – and you've filled your day with a shrill and disturbing noise.

And though it may sometimes seem like a small act, done from a far distance, we all have large antennas, and each of our actions can be far-reaching in its impact.

There's one problem, though. Now that I've actually come to enjoy and appreciate this little automatic car starter, my husband – and four-year-old son – are hoping to teach me how to work all those other electronic contraptions...

∽ *Every act you do – big or little – pushes a button, causing a far-reaching impact.*

In G-d's Treasure Chest

I'm not sure what spurred it, but this morning, during my prayers, my mind wandered.

Maybe it was because I was in the midst of teaching a five-part series on prayer. Or maybe it was simply the hope of stretching out the prayers because of the list of tasks and chores that awaited me once I concluded.

Whatever the case, my contemplation led me to some serious questioning about prayer. My mind wondered: Do You, G-d, really hear my prayers? Do my prayers have any significance or meaning to You? How could they? If You are truly the Master and Creator of all, as I had just mouthed from the prayer book, why would You care for or need my humble expressions of my feelings toward You? How could the stream of words exiting my mouth, some with deliberation, some just stumbling carelessly out amid thoughts of deadlines at work, an appointment I need to arrange, or the button I need to sew on my daughter's blouse, possibly be of worth to You?

With these thoughts, I concluded my prayers and began my workday. Soon I was working busily at my computer preparing a report that was due by the day's end.

Though an integral part of my life, I admit that I am no fan of computers. As much as computers help me, they never fail to frustrate me. And today was no exception.

I tried my best, but for some reason the Internet connection was down. If I got lucky, I was able to get connected only to lose the connection moments later as the whole system crashed. I soon realized that, with my lack of computer savvy, I was simply incapable of solving the problem on my own.

As frustration set in, I recalled once again my morning dilemma. To me, this was yet another proof, substantiating my point. If getting connected to just another computer over a phone line required such expertise and even the smallest problem — a virus, a line of code that needed updating, or a small glitch in the system — could ruin the connection, all the more so a connection with You, who is so infinitely apart and distant from me! Maybe a "prayer expert" could create a connection without any interference problems, but what could I possibly accomplish?

Late that evening, I wearily dragged myself off to bed after a full day. My early morning question returned as I was about to recite the Shema prayers. That was when I noticed something on my pillow.

Lying haphazardly was a small, crumpled white sheet of paper with colorful markings. In the center was a huge, misshapen orange-crayoned heart. Inside the heart, in my seven-year-old daughter's inimitable, partially legible handwriting, were purple letters forming this message: DEAR MOM, I LUV U. THANKS FOR BENG MY MOM.

As I read those ten crayoned words, the question that gnawed at me all day dissolved.

Did I need this card? Of course not. Why, I had bought the paper and crayons myself and given them to my daughter. After several days, when my daughter wouldn't notice, I would unobtrusively discard it, just like I had so many of her and her siblings' cards from the past. I try to keep some of their cards in a small treasure chest on my dresser, but eventually they reach their final resting place in the trash because no one has room for so much clutter.

But at that moment, this card was more beautiful than the most precious painting. It didn't bother me that the words were misshapen and spelled incorrectly. I didn't care that the purple and orange colors were a clashing eyesore. Nor did I consider how much thought or care she had put into it, or whether her behavior tomorrow would be in accordance with her fond message of love. Because, to me, none of those things mattered.

It meant the world to me that a seven-year-old girl who loves to draw took out a minute of her day to scribble some tender words on a paper. Gazing at the little scrap of paper lying on my pillow filled me with a warmth that was beyond explanation. My daughter's small note forged a bond of connection, appreciation, and love that was stronger than any glitches and interference could possibly disrupt — despite her lack of expertise, foresight, and artistry.

The next time I pray I will picture my words forming an offering of awkwardly crayoned words and forms on a piece of crumpled paper, expressing my deep love and longing to be connected with You. I will picture the large treasure chest that I am sure You must keep overflowing with all our prayers — even our most simple verbal scribbles. I will imagine You taking the time to tenderly read through our cards, made up from our tears, our innermost thoughts, hopeful wishes, and gratitude.

I have no doubt that You keep and treasure each of our tiniest offerings. After all, I'm sure You aren't worried about the clutter.

᠀ *G-d treasures each of our smallest offerings.*

Shadows in the Daytime

The other night, after tucking him in at bedtime, my youngest child called to me from his darkened bedroom. He was frightened.

"Look," he whispered hoarsely, his finger pointing toward the wall paralleling his bed. "Do you see them?"

Glancing in that direction, all I noticed was the usual pale, taupe wall. He was insistent, however, that grotesque figures were dancing on his wall, mocking and terrifying him. His fears sounded genuine, not merely the usual excuse to stay up a little longer.

It took me a few minutes to realize what was scaring my three-year-old.

"Watch carefully." I held up my five fingers, spreading them far apart and making a motion. Sure enough, a new dancing shape appeared on the wall.

Shadows — big ones, small ones, wide and narrow, tall and short — were disturbing my child. His own legs, arms, head, and bed pillow were collaborating to form this strange and scary scene that frightened him with his every move.

Just that day, late in the afternoon, we had been walking hand in hand along the sidewalk in front of our home. Then, he had been fascinated by these very same shadows. We had watched how in one direction we grew so tall and big, only to turn around and see ourselves grow so small, depending on the angle of the light. We stretched our arms out, making all kinds of shapes as we both broke into gales of laughter, observing our silly reflections.

My young son had felt so empowered, during the day, with his ability to create such interesting effects through his movements. Yet, somehow, at night those same funny shapes became objects of terror. The empowerment felt during the day became oppressing to him at night. His every movement had the power of instilling fear and arousing dread in his little heart.

And then it occurred to me how, in our own lives, the significance of the very same issues can change so drastically, depending on our circumstances and approach.

During the daytime of our lives, when we are standing upright and feel in control, our movements are empowering. Then the shadows in our lives are challenges to explore, experiences to broaden our horizons.

The scene drastically changes, however, when the evenings of our lives fall, when circumstances loom in blackness over us. During such difficult periods, we lie immobile and inactive as the very same shadows suddenly become points of terrible worry and anxiety.

As for my son and his insomnia, installing a small night-light did the trick. A little light dispels a great deal of darkness, and suddenly, though the shadows didn't disappear entirely, they became far less ominous.

   ✤ *Stand upright and act positively upon life's challenges, and you will feel empowered and enriched. Succumb to the fear of your darkness, and your every move will be frightening.*

*These journal questions reflect values from the
stories you just read. Record your answers for a greater
awareness of your spiritual perspective on life.*

On the Power of Deed
JOURNAL

1. What makes you feel valued?

2. What small gesture did you do for someone today?

3. Inspire someone who is sad by giving him or
    her hope.

4. Describe a situation where the passion of your words
    had a greater impact than the words themselves.

5. Take a moment before you pray to contemplate
    the potency of your prayers.

6. Describe a situation where a small act had a
    profound impact.

7. How has a challenge in your life been empowering at
    the same time as it filled you with anxiety?

III. Faith and Acceptance

ON LETTING GO
ON FINDING FAITH
ON FINDING G-D

The chassidic master Rebbe Nachman of Breslov said:

*"If you believe that things can be ruined,
you should believe that things can be repaired."*

*Don't resign yourself to gloom or failure.
Keep a positive picture on the possibility of
progress and beauty.*

On Letting Go

It's in Your Hands

I t was a professional party organizer's nightmare. Except that I am not a professional party planner, and this wasn't a party. A nightmare it most definitely was.

The event was scheduled for a Monday evening and was one of our institute's main yearly programs. It would be a catered affair that had been planned months ahead and would launch our new winter semester of educational programs and courses. Hundreds of people were expected to attend, and we were slated to have a special guest speaker from abroad and a musical interlude for entertainment.

Thursday afternoon, just four days before the event, I was checking off my mental to-do list to ascertain that no detail had been neglected. Centerpieces, color-coordinated table wear, tall elegant candles, and matching candlesticks had all been arranged. I heaved a sigh of relief as I gave myself a mental pat on the back that everything was so well under control.

But moments later I lifted the phone receiver to hear the dismaying news. "I'm very sorry, Mrs. Weisberg. I am not quite sure how it happened," the official-sounding, nasal voice began, "but apparently we've double-booked our hall for Monday night. I hate to do this to you, but I'm afraid you'll have to find another venue."

I summoned all of my persuasive powers to convince the woman on the other end of the phone line that this was simply not possible. She, not I, would have to find another location, and our program would have to go on as planned. I begged, I pleaded, I threatened. I spoke diplomatically and patiently, and I shouted loudly and angrily. I tried every tactic, to no avail. I demanded to speak to this woman's superior, and I contacted influential board members. Finally, late Friday morning I realized that my efforts were futile and my time would be better spent scrambling for an alternative.

Fortunately, a short while later, I was able to find another hall to book, quite some distance away. Now I had to tackle the major problem of informing everyone of the change of location. Needless to say, I was a bundle of nerves attacking the phones, trying to contact as many prospective participants to avoid an utter disaster for the coming Monday night.

Amid all this, my four-year-old arrived home from school. His mother's frantic expression didn't faze him. He ran straight over to me, clutching something in his arms, and burst into tears. Thrusting the small object at me, his face fell as he tearfully said, "Look!" He handed me a colorful arts and craft paper from school. "I made this especially for you. But now it tore!"

I looked at his pitiful expression and tried to console him, telling him that I really liked it just the way it was. He wouldn't hear of it. "No! It's ripped and now it's all ruined," he whimpered.

I hugged him tightly as he released a torrent of tears until I began to feel him relax in my arms, confident that I would find some magical solution for him. I ventured, "Honey, don't worry. It's not ruined. I'll get the tape, and we'll fix it all up just like new."

His eyes widened, and he smiled as I got the glue and tape and we fixed up his creation to look even better than before.

It took us all of about six minutes from the moment his tearful face walked through the front door to his heaving then relaxing cries on my shoulder until finally a radiant smile broke across his features and he ran happily along to his other waiting toys.

But somehow, as I returned to my harried preparation, those six minutes refreshed my perspective of my own dilemma. Dialing the numbers on the phone pad, I reflected how often we try to make something special – a beautiful "craft" of our own making – just for You, G-d. It may be having extra guests for a special Shabbat or *yom tov* (holiday) dinner or coordinating a visitation to the hospital or homebound or an educational awareness program like I was now organizing – or any other "project" that we undertake to contribute to making the world just a little bit of a nicer place.

Sometimes, we work on these projects, crafting them with care, choosing judiciously the exact detailed particulars to make it most beautiful. And then, along the way something happens, and there is a tear in our fabric, a glitch in our efforts, a problem that becomes insurmountable. We want to present a beautiful, finished product, but it is torn, beyond repair. Perhaps You may be happy with our effort just as it is, but we wanted to craft something nicer, something almost perfect.

I learned two things from that little encounter with my son. First, I discovered the benefit of letting go with a good cry on Your shoulder and the comforting assurance that You are there with magical solutions to all my dilemmas.

I also learned not to get so carried away with my preparation for the project that I forget the point of the project and the recipient of the gift.

Was this about *my* project or Your present? Was I worried that my project, which I had worked on for months, would not be the success that I envisioned, or was it about presenting You with the best gift I could craft?

After all, if it was for You, You were a partner in its creation and equally responsible for its success. So if I've done my part, yet circumstances beyond my control still interfere, I can let go and invite Your magical assistance to fix up the tears and glitches.

Yes, I continued frantically dialing that Friday afternoon, but now with a new awareness. Now I could let go. My pent-up energy was released as I felt Your comforting arms around me.

Of course, this minor tale, which at the time seemed major, wouldn't be complete, just like my son's craft, without a happy ending.

The event did take place that Monday evening. It was the coldest day of our winter yet. But the new hall was lavish and far more luxurious than the original one. It was warmed by the hundreds of warm hearts in the full-capacity crowd that attended, probably, in great part, due to the many calls and reminders. The music was elegant and inviting, the food was delicious, and the guest speaker was enchanting, leaving the audience inspired to make You a greater part of their lives.

In short, the program progressed smoothly without another single glitch, and all those who were present remarked how that evening felt, well, almost magical.

The following day, after the tension lifted, as I was describing the event to my husband, my son climbed up on my lap, touched my lips, and said, "I like it so much when you smile, Mommy."

"And I, too, like it when you smile," I replied.

❧ *When situations loom out of your control, resign yourself to the control of the One greater than you.*

The Missing Earring

On the first day of Pesach, as I reached into the top right corner of my jewelry box to fetch my special pair of earrings, my hand returned empty. I rummaged around the back of the jewelry box in case my earrings had dropped into a concealed crevice. I ran my fingers over every small compartment in the box. I scrutinized the top surface of my dresser as well as every small container near my jewelry box. I groped inside all the drawers throughout my bedroom – all to no avail. My earrings had vanished.

Of course I was upset; after all, this was my favorite pair of earrings, worn solely on special occasions. Moreover, those earrings had personal sentimental value, presented to me by my husband commemorating our anniversary. I noticed the tender care he used in choosing this pair. They were just his taste, as well as mine – delicate white gold shapes, with tiny clasps of yellow gold, surrounded by linear, perfectly aligned square diamonds. Understated and refined elegance.

Almost equally disturbing was the unrest it caused within. My belongings are usually well organized, especially now, after an intense pre-Pesach cleanup. Yet this threw my calm order out of balance. I couldn't help but question what else was out of order. Why hadn't I noticed my misplaced earrings in the immense cleanup? Had I neglected some other area of my home?

My initial response to my predicament was, of course, to blame myself. I had been careless and not vigilant enough. Mentally, I went over the times that I had worn these earrings, and I hunted inside the pockets of possible outfits where I might have accidentally misplaced them. I checked my desktop to see if perhaps I had haphazardly taken them off while on the phone.

My next reaction was to blame those around me. Maybe one of my children had thought it would be fun to "play" with Mommy's precious present. Or maybe I had instructed one of my youngsters to put the earrings away, and the child had gotten sidetracked in the process. I searched through my children's rooms. I looked through their dressers, their boxes, and their toy containers — with no success.

Disconcerting, too, was that over the last several days I had had many workers coming through my home. One had polished the wooden floors, another had installed a new counter top, and then there was the carpet cleaner. I admit to secretly suspecting that my earrings may have been pocketed by some lucky worker, even though rationally I knew that none had even come close to my bedroom.

Finally, after retracing all possible places and doing a thorough search of any possible location and lots of mental blaming of me and others, an acceptance finally set in. It really wasn't a tragedy, and it was simply meant to be.

Sure, the question of what else was misplaced still nagged at me, but even that began to subside. My earrings would be found if it was meant to be, and the situation was beyond my control.

This insignificant incident was small enough for me to apply it to the many bigger situations in life when we have a dream or goal that is "lost" or goes "missing." It upsets our plan of organization, of how we feel our life and world "ought" to be. It upsets our careful cleanup, our meticulous plotting and arranging of what goes where and how neatly organized our life should be. Suddenly this uncalled for change of direction makes us realize that we are not in charge.

Our reaction to these sudden losses of dreams, goals, or plans is manifold. First, we usually search our ways to determine if all is in order. This is healthy self-evaluation and productive reorganization.

But then we sometimes progress to the next, unconstructive step – becoming obsessed with the loss, blaming ourselves irrationally, and incriminating others accusatorially. Comes a time when we have to reach an acceptance that, for reasons beyond our control or awareness, the situation was simply meant to be.

And sometimes, unexpectedly, with that acceptance may come the solution to our missing goal or dream.

Like a few days later when I opened up my jewelry box to discover my special earrings, in their proper spot. "Hey, I am so happy!" I jubilantly exclaimed to my children. "Who found my lost earrings?"

Apparently, my oldest daughter had spotted my missing earrings in my youngest child's room, where they were nestling on his bookshelf and, knowing how distraught I was, was pleased to return them to their rightful location.

The exact path that my earrings journeyed en route to my son's room still remains a mystery – one which I don't care to unravel. Mystifying as well is the fact that I checked my son's room, as well as this bookshelf, several times. How this obvious spot missed my vigilant search still eludes me.

But once I reached an acceptance of my situation, that it was beyond my control and just meant to be – the solution was at hand.

༄ *Despite your careful plotting of your goals, aspirations, or dreams, there are times when you need to let go – without blame or bitterness.*

Baby Talk

"Little beings like us talking to G-d! Does He really need it, or even listen?"

"Will G-d change His mind and His grand plan just because I asked Him to?"

"Of course G-d knows what we want — He knows everything — so isn't it strange that we have to verbalize it? Two or three times a day, no less!"

These were some of the comments going around the table.

It was the first night of an eight-week series that I was conducting on prayer. I had asked the participants to think about some of the questions they had and what areas of prayer they would like to explore in the course.

After the initial awkward moments of a group of strangers packed into a room together, the conversation began to flow easily. I nodded, encouraging the class participants to voice their thoughts before we began studying from the sources.

But, truth be told, my own thoughts were somewhere else entirely.

Nodding vacantly to the conversation, my mind was replaying the scene, earlier that evening, of my six-month-old baby bursting into tears as she realized I was heading out the front door to come to this class. Her pudgy little hands, which but moments before were flapping about eagerly, anticipating my reaching out and cuddling her, were tensed in frustration; her legs kicked angrily, and pitiful cries were issuing from her mouth.

Babies have a way of communicating clearly and openly. It's not until years later that we learn the skill of hiding our thoughts and veiling our true feelings. A baby will actively — and loudly — demonstrate, with her entire being, her likes and dislikes, the things she appreciates and the things that she objects to.

It's heartwarming to watch my daughter's face break into the largest smile as I lift her from her crib after a nap or feel her cuddle lovingly against me as I play with her. Tonight the vision of a distressed Sara Leah, hands outstretched expectantly, wouldn't go away.

I was mentally planning how, next time, I would slip out through the front door while she was distracted by her toys in the back room. *That should prevent the guilt-provoking wails*, I thought as I caught the last sentence of the conversation around me.

"I understand that praying forges a connection with G-d. But will He only fulfill my requests if I say them?"

We had reached the end of the table, and heads were nodding in agreement to the comments of the last participant.

Eyes were now turned expectantly to me.

And just at that very moment, as my mind was working to fade out the vision of my young daughter's crestfallen face, its relevance to the discussion at hand suddenly hit me.

I heard myself explain how prayer is basically G-d asking us to tell Him how things look from *our* perspective. He gives us the opportunity a few times a day, or any time that we need to, to share with Him how things look from down here — from *our* point of view.

G-d is good, and therefore everything He does is only goodness. But that's from *His* perspective, seeing and realizing what needs to be accomplished in our world, seeing how all the pieces of the puzzles of our lives fit together.

But from our perspective, looking at those individual pieces of the puzzle that we're stuck with — and living through — sometimes things look awfully disappointing and difficult.

Here's where my baby comes in.

I can explain and explain to her how important it is for me to occasionally leave her, that I'll be back so soon, how one day she'll understand and realize that these short absences were *good* things, not tragedies. But for now, as I walk out the door, she is inconsolable. To her, her world is crumbling.

I know, of course, that I am her mother, and I know far better than she what's good and what's bad. Obviously her separation anxiety won't prevent me from leaving when I need to, and her cries won't stop me from doing something for her benefit — even if she dislikes it. After all, she's just a baby, with no real understanding of the workings of our world.

But despite all that, when she does wail in frustration or despair, I recognize that she's showing me how lousy things are from *her* perspective. She's communicating to me how much something is bothering her.

Whether or not her small, limited view of reality is a valid one is irrelevant. To her, her pain is real.

So although I will still need to leave her at times, although I won't be able to stop her from crying in every situation, I'll do whatever I can to make any possible accommodations in my general plans in order that she not become too distraught. Maybe I'll try to distract her with her toys when she confronts something unpleasant. Maybe I'll give her an extra hug before I go and after I return.

The same applies to the positive feedback I get from her. The smiles that break out across her face when I hold her don't make me love her more — I already love her, utterly and absolutely, regardless of how much love she shows me back. I also know that she enjoys it when I play with her, whether or not she communicates her delight with her gurgles or her giggles. But the more she does gurgle and giggle, the more she does show me her joy in loving me, the more I'll go to all lengths to keep her smiling and joyful.

I'll make every effort to take *her* perspective into account, and I'll try to arrange things so that her view and mine better coincide. I'll calibrate my actions so that they will elicit more positive and less negative feedback from her — even while still sticking to my grand plan of what needs to be done.

Not always will I succeed in completely satisfying her from her perspective, but I sure will try.

It is true that G-d doesn't need our prayers, that He fully understands our wants and needs far better than we do, that He appreciates what we are experiencing without our verbalizing it.

But if I seek and respond to my baby's feedback, imagine how important the feedback of our perspective on the good and bad in our lives is — to the Infinite One.

    ✋ *G-d understands your needs far better than you do, but still seeks your input and prayers to make things good – from your perspective.*

The Ultimate Editor

As a writer, I've come to realize the importance of a good editor.

Every journal or publication has one. He or she is the person who guards the mandate for the publication. The person who decides which articles will see the light of day and which do not fit into the parameters of what's acceptable and who suggests/insists on the changes to be made in the content and wording.

I've also come to see that there are varying calibers and styles in editors.

There are those editors who edit too loosely. They give free rein to their authors, leaving mistakes, abstruse sentences, or plain old weak writing unchecked. Lacking vision, they neglect to establish a concrete focus for their publication. Creativity thrives, but chaos abounds.

Then there are those editors who edit too stringently. They consistently delete whole paragraphs, replace your ideas and expressions with their own, until the original piece becomes hardly recognizable. The finished product might read perfectly, but it has practically become the editor's creation instead of yours.

What differentiates the really top-notch editor from the mediocre is the rare knack of setting strong guidelines while at the same time allowing the unique talent and flavor of each author to shine through.

The ideal editor may be a great writer himself. He may, theoretically, have been able to express the same ideas and feelings presented in the article you've submitted "better" than you have. But he understands his writers' need to author their independent creations. And he also understands that allowing his writers to express themselves in their own different and varied ways will result in a better article and a better publication.

So though he will polish, weed out, and improve, discarding, replacing, and adding words, ideas, or sentences in accordance with his established criteria and grand plan, he'll make sure to maintain the unique style of the author throughout. He'll choose the author's words and expressions over his own — even while correcting or enhancing.

He'll work together with the author to develop a piece that is on track, watching that it doesn't lose focus and become sidetracked from its goal — even while allowing the author's exploration along the way.

    ❧ ☙

In life, we are presented with many choices. In these choices we become authors of our destiny.

Every path we tread, every turn we take, composes a fresh new sentence, paragraph, or chapter in our lives. These combine to develop into our unique life stories, worded with our contributions and innovations, styled by our special personality and talents, and marked with our mistakes and slipups.

And throughout it all, our ultimate Editor is overseeing our project, watching carefully that we don't get sidetracked from our true mandate and goal, helping us to realize which choices might work better — while still permitting us free choice. Despite His munificent guidelines and guidance to get us to our end goal, He enables us to find our own voice and to author our unique creation.

Because He knows that's the way to get from us the very best story we can deliver.

> ❧ *While you are presented with many choices on how to structure your life, realize that your ultimate "Editor" is making sure you don't forget your mandate altogether.*

The Crumb on
My Kitchen Floor

There are moments in life when I feel like...the crumb on my kitchen floor.

Like the useless crumb, my life seems almost purposeless, my contribution to the greater whole nil. I roll about aimlessly, awaiting the butt of the broom to toss me to an ignoble destiny.

Like that crumb, I feel more like a nuisance than a contributor. I while away my time, assuming no responsibility for the future. I am pushed here and shoved there, stepped on at times, merely being influenced or trampled on by my environment, but in no position to have control over it.

I just sit there, aimlessly watching life go on around me.

Then there are moments in life when I feel like...an airplane pilot.

I am on top of the world, literally. Nothing impedes or forces my path. Exhilarated by the speed, intoxicated by the distances I traverse, I grasp the rudder of life and progress to my chosen destinations —

which are utterly mine to choose.

I am the master of my destiny, deciding where to go, how to get there, and what to accomplish.

When I've had a good day – if I've delivered an interesting lecture that had the participants excited, if I've received a gracious compliment on my work, or if I've had a great discussion with one of my kids or my husband – I'll feel like the airplane pilot.

But then, when I've had a bad day – something didn't go well at work or a child is sick or I've had an argument with my husband or my creative juices just don't flow – then I'll feel like the crumb on my kitchen floor.

બ   ૭

Two very extreme feelings – the worthless crumb and the triumphant flyer. Which is the real me? Is either perspective real or true? Pondering these thoughts and vacillating between both emotions, I watched my young son play one afternoon, captivated by his computer car racing game.

"Look how fast I can drive," he enthused.

"Great," I replied. "But why don't you steer the car that way?" I pointed to a shortcut, crossing out of the intended path.

He paused in his game to explain. "No, Ma. You see, I can stop or start or go fast or slow. I can steer." He demonstrated these actions with his car. "But I can't go off the path." Twisting the joystick, he showed me his futile attempt to veer too much off the lanes marked on the screen. "See, it doesn't let me go off track."

The thought then occurred to me that our lives cannot really be viewed from on top of the world, like a flyer in his cockpit, nor from underfoot, as a crumb on the floor. I think that a truer, more correct perspective is that of the small racing car driver in my child's computer game.

As the racing car driver races down the track of life, his path is clearly marked for him. Road signs show him where to turn and how to progress. There is a beginning, an end, a route to be taken, a distance to be covered.

The next time I feel the haughtiness of the flyer, I'll try to remember that my destiny, too, is tracked out for me. You, G-d, have plotted my path and chosen my course and are at my side, watching and constantly guiding.

But when I feel like the powerless crumb on my floor, I'll try to remind myself that You have empowered me to steer my way through this course — to decide how fast or slow to travel, how sharply or gently to navigate the curves, when to pause and when to surge forward. You have entrusted to me the choice of whether I stop in defeat and succumb to life's obstacles or forge ahead, undeterred by life's turns and bumps.

You've even built in safety bumpers along the path to help me take the sharper bends — and survive the crashes. You've made allowances for falling off the road and provided a built-in system for me to find my way back, onto the track.

You've done all that. But in the end, whether or not I get to the finish line successfully is entirely up to me.

 ᠅ *Don't lose sight of your true position in life. While your destiny is determined, you are empowered to choose your attitude and approach.*

*These journal questions reflect values from the
stories you just read. Record your answers for a greater
awareness of your spiritual perspective on life.*

On Letting Go
JOURNAL

1. Make a list of five things that are beyond your control.

2. Describe a situation when you "let go" that had a positive ending. Describe how you felt.

3. Take five minutes today to thank G-d for taking care of all those things in your life that you do not control.

4. Picture yourself falling back into a pillow of faith and acceptance. How does it feel?

5. How much of a role do you feel "destiny" and "free choice" each play in your life?

6. Describe a situation where something beyond your control ended positively. How was the negative part only a small piece of the ultimately larger, beautiful puzzle?

On Finding Faith

WHY?

The question that I face most often in my life is, "Why?"
This little, three-letter word always holds a world of curiosity. Sometimes it is accompanied by pain; almost inevitably, it contains a dose of frustration.

This small word plagues me constantly.

I hear it emanating from deep within. Sometimes, I hear it from my cynical voice after a particularly overwhelming or tiring day. Sometimes, it originates from a place of sorrow after encountering a tragedy or hardship too difficult to bear.

I'm always hearing "why" from my children. Ranging in age from newborn to eighteen years, this question comes in all shapes — from why one has to put on an extra sweater to why he must finish his dinner before snacking to why her bedtime is so much earlier than "all" her other classmates.

I hear "why" from my husband, too. Why can't he leave his books or papers spread over the dining room table? Why do plans have to be organized so well in advance?

And I hear "why" from my adult students at my Institute of Jewish Studies almost every time I deliver a class or lecture. Why do married Orthodox women have to cover their hair? Why can't we flick on a light switch on Shabbat? Why can't we wear clothing containing a mixture of wool and linen?

I like to pride myself on the fact that I usually have calm, rational, and enlightening responses to these queries. I might sit my children down to a long explanation on how nutritious, well-balanced meals and sufficient sleep is important for healthy, physical well-being. I might convince my husband of the advantages of orderliness or how being organized helps to find things later when they are needed. And I might explain to my students the beauty of the Jewish value of modesty or how refraining from creative work can rejuvenate us for the entire week ahead.

But every so often these rational explanations don't work. I'll explain and explain until I'm blue in the face only to encounter yet another barrage of counterarguments. I'll sometimes be drawn into a long discussion with one of my children which turns into an explosive argument and we land at square one, with each of us not having moved an inch toward the other's perspective.

At those times, I have to calculate how much the said gain is worth. If I decide it is important enough, I've learned, from experience, that rather than trying to convince my husband or children of the obvious merits of my sensible thinking to simply answer, "Honey, please, do it just for me."

So I won't convince my husband how nice the mahogany dining-room table looks bare and gleaming because he obviously doesn't appreciate that. He sees it instead as a viable option for storage, and no discussion will convince him differently. But if every time he refrains from leaving his papers on the table he is demonstrating to me how much he cares about my wants and how important I am in his life, the entire picture changes. He is willing to make such sacrifices for me.

And I won't convince my child why he needs an extra sweater because, though I am feeling chilly, he obviously is not. But he will agree to "do Mommy a favor." Because, after all, that's just a small way to show his appreciation for all the many things that Mom does for him.

As for my students or the cynical voice within me, when rational arguments just won't answer the incessant "why," I'll resort to answering, "Because this is how G-d wants it."

So though I don't understand why I can't buy that elegant European suit of wool and linen, hey, if it pleases You, I'll do without. After all, it's the least I can do to show You, G-d, my gratitude for all the good that You shower upon me.

At first I used to think that such a response to my children, husband, or students was a cop-out. How could any self-respecting woman resort to sounding so squeamishly emotional?

But then I realized that while such a response does not emphasize the rational merits of my argument, it underlines why, in fact, I am having the discussion to begin with. It brings to light the very core of the relationship between me and my children or husband, and between me or my students and G-d, irrespective of the specific issue at hand.

Or, in other words, it brings to the surface a far greater bond between us that reaches deep down to our essential connection, a connection that is so deep it surpasses even logic.

While the rational is limited to each individual's experience and conception of reality, this touches the infinite bond between me and my children, me and my husband, and us and G-d.

And that bond is not something that any circumstance or any argument – or any question of "why" – can ever interfere with.

᠀ *When you can't fathom the need for a particular favor, do it despite your reluctance. Do it because your most profound bond to another surpasses even the rational.*

A Bouquet of Roses

L ike most women, I love flowers.

My favorite is a dozen or more long-stemmed, freshly cut red roses. But a bouquet of any brilliant assortment with its exquisite aroma — whether orchids, petunias, or birds of paradise — always brings a smile to my face.

My husband knows of this weakness of mine. He uses it to his advantage whenever he wants to win my heart or gain forgiveness for any of the misdeeds that husbands are so well known for.

The other evening, as my husband was heading out the front door, I reminded him of his promise to be back promptly at 7:30. I was teaching a class at eight o'clock and had some errands to take care of beforehand. I impressed upon him the need for me to leave on time as I urged him not to lose sight of his watch or become sidetracked.

At exactly 7:31, I was waiting impatiently by the front door, peering down the block for our gray van. By 7:45, I was pacing frantically up and down my front corridor nervously eyeing the clock, and by 7:53, when my husband finally sauntered up our front steps, I could barely contain myself.

Thrusting an exquisite bouquet into my arms, he explained how he had passed a stand selling especially beautiful flowers. Proudly he announced, knowing how much I love flowers, that he had decided to stop and was a "little delayed" in the process.

Had I not been as rushed as I was, I would have found my tongue and, contrary to my husband's perception, would have expressed just how enraged I was. Instead, wordlessly, I grabbed the keys, dumped the flowers, and stormed out the door.

Shelving my plans for any errands, and skipping a few stop signs along the way, I arrived at my lecture, nerves ravaged, just in the nick of time.

After a few moments, I calmed down and could actually teach. The many participants were, as usual, from a wide variety of backgrounds. As the class came to its conclusion, one student, Diane, asked why organized religion was so vital. "Why not just feel G-d in our hearts? After all, what is the need for all the dos and don'ts of Judaism?"

I thought for a moment. Suddenly the analogy struck me.

I relayed to the women the evening's events prior to my arrival at the class. I asked if they thought I was justified in being upset with my husband's purchase.

I was certain of their response. Of course they thought such behavior was completely uncalled for.

"But why?" I questioned. "What was wrong with him doing something he thought I would like?"

Diane articulated what some of the others were thinking. "You told him that you *needed* him home on time, and he totally disregarded it. He was too self-absorbed to understand your perspective, your need to be on time. He just doesn't get it."

"Yes, but he came late in order to buy me a present. Doesn't that prove his love?" I was playing devil's advocate.

Diane was insistent. "True, he wanted to please you. But it was on *his* terms, not yours. He was foregoing your explicit wish and need in order to do something that he imagined you would enjoy."

"I guess that is what the Torah is all about," I explained. "G-d tells us *His* terms. What He needs from our relationship. Sure, we can by-pass His wishes — and even do something wonderful and benevolent. We may even have Him in mind. But ultimately, isn't that acting on our own terms, disregarding His?

"We may not always understand what the Torah wants from us. But the Torah is G-d's explicit communication with us, telling us, This is what I need. This is what is important to Me. Don't just act on your own volition. *This* is what you can do to have a relationship with Me.

"Maybe it doesn't make sense to you. Maybe you understand. Maybe, you don't. But this is what I want you to do."

When I came home later that evening, the roses were adeptly arranged in a crystal vase on the kitchen table. By the foot of the vase lay a small card.

It was a sincere apology note.

I guess even husbands sometimes do get it.

❧ *We may do the nicest deed, but if it isn't with the other in mind, it remains a selfish act.*

Why Do We Smile to Ourselves?

I'm sure she did it today.

I've been watching in anticipation, awaiting it for the last few weeks. And today it happened.

Today, my newborn baby looked me straight in the eye with her huge, innocent eyes — and smiled. It was a full, toothless grin, flaunting her round, dimpled cheeks and demonstrating that she finally knows who I am. For weeks I'd cuddled her, spoken to her, rocked her on my shoulder, cooed to her, and sang to her, and today she acknowledged that she recognizes me. She smiled back.

A friendly smile in passing greeting. A full, guttural laugh. These are ways that we humans communicate with one another. It is how we share our joy, kinship, and friendship with each other.

Until today, my newborn baby, Sara Leah, communicated only through her crying. Babies cry... and wail...and cry some more. That is how they convey their discomfort — their hunger, their pain, their tiredness, their need to be changed or just held and coddled.

Our response to a baby's crying is automatic. Sara Leah will begin to cry and immediately a slew of little hands — ranging from my five-year-old son all the way up to my teenage children — will surround her, all eager to pick her up and stop her screams. Invariably my children's next question will be "Does she want to eat now, Mommy? What's bothering her? Why is she crying?"

But crying is a baby's very effective way of communicating. The more upset she sounds, the more we'll attempt one thing after another just to curtail her distressing wails.

A silent tear. Bitter weeping. Hysterical sobs. These are ways that, from infancy onward, we share with each other our sadness and sorrow, our pain and discomfort, our frustrations and disappointments.

Our tears and our sobs draw empathy. Our smiles and our laughter elicit happiness. Tears and laughter — each conveys feelings on opposite ranges of the emotional spectrum. Yet both are our means of reaching out to another, often more powerfully than any spoken word. After we've shared our joys and our sorrows, we feel better. It is how we communicate our need for a response — be it empathy, support, or just kinship.

But then there are those times when we laugh or cry alone. We've received good news and, overflowing with happiness, we can't help but laugh out loud — even though no one is present to hear it. And then there are times when we've experienced an overwhelming hurt — too personal and deep to share with another — and we retreat in solitude, our heart torn to pieces, overcome with sobs.

But if, from earliest infancy, we cry and smile as a form of communication, to whom are we communicating with these solitary tears and smiles?

Perhaps these tears and smiles indicate that even in our aloneness we aren't ever really alone. That even in our solitude, we realize that we are sharing the deepest of our emotions. Intuitively, we understand that we are being heard — by the One who hears and sees all cries and smiles.

After experiencing a tragedy beyond our comprehension, the

lonely tears cascading down our cheeks is our way of protesting to You, of beseeching You to put an end to our suffering. Or, as good fortune smiles our way and a grin forms across our features, it is our way of acknowledging our gratitude to You for all the good You shower on us.

From the very beginning of our lives, we use our smiles and our tears to communicate. Sometimes, it is our silent but powerful way of sharing with another person.

And sometimes — whether it is our intention or not — it is our truest way of expressing that deep down we realize: we are never alone.

    ❧ *As you smile or as you cry, realize that you are never alone in your joy or in your sorrow.*

The Dance of Love

A friend of mine recently gave birth to a baby boy. This child was not my friend's first, but was born after a handful of other wonderful, talented, and healthy children.

This past Sunday afternoon, I attended the brit milah (circumcision) celebration. There were many other well-wishers celebrating in the birth and joy of a new life.

But the celebration was a bittersweet one; the newborn baby was born with Down's syndrome.

We all stood solemnly in the shul listening to the blessings ushering the baby into the covenant of Abraham, our forefather. At the conclusion of the blessings we all wished "*mazal tov!*" to the parents and the many relatives present. Soon a joyous song and dance broke out, attracting, like a magnet, more and more into its circle.

There was an undercurrent of raw emotion in the large room. Entranced, I watched the circle of dancers and the smiling onlookers who clapped along.

I noticed one woman's husband dancing around and around. I knew that this man was battling a life-threatening illness.

Another in the circle was a father whose child was severely physically challenged. His wife stood a few rows behind me. She wore a gentle smile on her lips, but her deep-set eyes revealed the story of her trials.

A close friend and confidante was also present, observing and smiling. I knew that she had been trying futilely to have a child of her own.

More and more continued to join, and as the circle turned, I noticed a man who had recently lost his job and was in dire financial straits.

These were but a few of the people present. I was sure that many others were also carrying in their hearts their own little package of sorrow, their own little bundle of pain.

As I stood watching, the rhythm of the happy song overtook me, becoming the dance and rhythm of life itself in which we were all taking part as we expressed our thanks to our Creator.

And as I studied the scene, I thought how we humans are endowed with such an enormous range of emotions. I marveled at the depth and intensity of love one can feel for a child, for a spouse, for a parent. I wondered how this immensity of feeling can be contained within such finite beings. Yet our emotions assert themselves constantly, almost having a life of their own, full of texture and depth, full of cravings, wants, and desires.

They are real; they feel real. From the happiness of a gentle, graceful moment to the despair of a dark hour overshadowed by grief.

If only I could capture and preserve forever the lightness of pure and undiluted joy, hope or happiness! If I could only throw a switch that would stop the floods of sadness, frustration, and sorrow!

But watching the circle, I saw how we cannot stop the torrents of feelings. Instead, we all ride the roller coaster of life, loving the moments on the top but aware with certainty that these will plunge, too, to moments of struggles as the ride of life races forward.

And as I watched, I thought about the commandment to love

You, our G-d, unconditionally, with the entire range of our feelings, with all our might, all our passions, and all of our selves.

I thought how this love is revealed each time, despite what You put us through. Despite the difficulties and struggles. Despite the depth of anger, frustration, and despair. Despite the heaviness and the pain. Despite how our moments of gratification and joy far too rapidly become tinged with loss and despair.

Despite the apparent unfairness of life.

Despite knowing all this, and feeling it even deeper.

Despite all this, we take this whole mixed bag, the whole gamut of emotions – the positives and the negatives, the happiness and the hurt, the goodness and the grief – and we still present it all to You as we dance around and around in the circle of life, singing and celebrating our love to You.

Is a greater form of unconditional love possible?

∽ *Underneath the difficulties you endure, uncover the inherent faith that G-d loves you and cares for you.*

These journal questions reflect values from the stories you just read. Record your answers for a greater awareness of your spiritual perspective on life.

On Finding Faith
JOURNAL

1. What does faith mean to you?

2. When is the last time you spoke to G-d and confided your inner thoughts, dreams, and wishes?

3. Do an act today that you don't ordinarily do. Do it just because you think G-d will be happy with this act.

4. How do you express your unconditional love for G-d?

5. Describe a situation when, through your tears, or through your joy, you felt you were not alone in your grief or in your happiness.

6. How can a nice deed sometimes remain a selfish act?

On Finding G-d

Hide-and-Seek

One bright, sunny afternoon, I sat watching my two children playing a lively game of hide-and-seek.

My younger daughter Shira was the first to be the seeker, and as she counted to twenty, the older one, Naomi, ran to hide. Naomi had discovered a very creative hiding spot, one that would be difficult for Shira to detect.

Meanwhile, Shira finished her countdown and began scurrying off all over the house in a wild search. She searched and she searched, in small corners and large, to no avail.

The silent moments ticked by, and Shira's search was becoming more desperate. Lines of anxiety were forming on her small forehead. My usually very persistent daughter almost seemed ready to admit defeat.

In despair, Shira called out to Naomi, hoping to get some response to clue her in on her sister's whereabouts. Silence reigned.

Then Shira turned, as if struck by a new idea, and optimistically headed off, only to get sidetracked along the way by the subtlest sound of a shifting of legs on the wooden floor. Her ears perked up, and she stopped in her tracks. She made a sharp U-turn to search in the opposite direction and seconds later discovered her sister's ingenious location.

Shira leaped at Naomi, and both laughed aloud, reunited. The two shared a moment of closeness, admiring Naomi's ingenuity in thinking of such a location and Shira's in discovering it. For that blithe moment, they enjoyed each other thoroughly, and you would think the two were forever the best of friends, never experiencing the normal squabbling between siblings.

Watching my youngsters play, my mind wandered to You, G-d. I thought of how, so often, You seem to be hiding Yourself from us. From afar You watch, allowing us to run here and there bereft of direction. The lines of sorrow and anxiety form on our temples as we wonder whether we will ever find You.

Sometimes, despite our perseverance as a nation, we're almost ready to give up. Sometimes we do give up. We trail off in all the wrong directions, despairing of ever making You a meaningful part of our lives.

But always You make some noise. Sometimes it's a slight ruffling sound. Sometimes it's louder. Some event in our personal lives, or in our national lives, catches our attention, drawing us back to where we are meant to be. You help us to rediscover You, and we feel closer to You.

For those moments in history, we are reunited, surer of our direction.

The sounds of my children reorganizing for another round of hide-and-seek interrupted my reverie. This time my four-year-old son, Yisroel, begged to be included. The round began exactly as before. This time, though, my older children were patronizing Yisroel, pretending not to locate him in his obvious hiding spot. Eventually, however, they came over to him and laughingly declared, "We found you!"

Yisroel's response? Simple. He put his hands over his eyes and victoriously announced, "No, you didn't. You can't find me!" He stayed like that for several seconds, ignoring their claims and comments. After all, he reasoned, if he couldn't see them, they simply weren't there.

This brought my thoughts back to You again. How often in life do we act like a little child, pretending You aren't there? We cover our eyes, denying You appropriate entry into our lives, even while, deep down, we know that You are right before us. How silly we must appear to You.

Several more rounds of hide-and-seek were played, and it was time to call a close to the game.* First, though, we all had to even the score.

True, there were times throughout our exile that we acted like a silly child, closing our eyes and denying You access. We pretend that You are not there, feigning ignorance, rejecting You as the guiding force in all that we do.

But then again, You did hide in such difficult, remote spots. Far too many times, these places were impossibly unfair for our limited capabilities. How could You expect us to find You?

So, taking all this into account, I think that must make the score just about even now. How about we call it a tie and finally end the game?

> ✒ *Sometimes, like a young child, we pretend G-d is not a part of our lives. Denying G-d entry into our lives is denying a part of ourselves.*

---

* The metaphor of comparing our state of exile to a game is found in the works of Rabbi Dov Ber, the Maggid of Mezeritch (second leader of the chassidic movement, d. 1772).

The Caretaker

My home backs onto a small elementary school. I love to watch for the first signs of activity each morning as I busy myself in my kitchen overlooking the sprawling grounds. I survey the children scurrying along as they line up to enter the building. Several moments later the few latecomers will straddle in.

In the afternoons, my youngest son and I will spy on the children at recess playing ball games or climbing the bars. In the winter, they frolic in the snow, and in the spring, boisterous boys splash in the puddles. Later, we'll watch the building emptying as the children run off to the waiting cars of parents or caregivers. The yard then becomes silent and desolate.

One figure, however, always remains.

The school caretaker arrives in the early hours of dawn, just as my morning coffee begins to percolate. Soon I see him working in the yard, picking up papers. On snowy, blistery mornings, he'll be bundled in his bulky snowsuit, pushing the large snowblower back and forth along the winding walkways. Then he'll lift his heavy shovel to reach the narrower crevices that his machine has overlooked.

The caretaker is still there at the end of the day, long after the children have departed. In the spring, he'll haul his oversized green garbage bag, picking up the tossed candy wrappers and miscellaneous papers that never reached their proper destination. He'll empty the many trash bins placed throughout the large campus and tend to the overgrown grass.

Often, when I peek through my window's shutters, long after it has grown dark outdoors, I'll again observe his familiar figure. Lights throughout the building will systematically switch on as his tall frame treks from room to room carrying his mop and pail. Sometimes, even late at night, I'll spot him locking up and firmly securing all the building's doors and windows.

I wonder if the schoolchildren pay any attention to their unobtrusive caretaker. When they scuttle across the clean walkway, do they stop to consider how many hours it took to clear it? As they carelessly toss their wrappers, do they pay heed to how yesterday's have miraculously disappeared? As they track mud across the school's hallways, do they remember how the floors once gleamed?

Do they greet their devoted caretaker with a smile in the morning? Do they know his name? Do they wave goodbye as they rush to the waiting cars in the afternoon?

I doubt they give him much notice or gratitude. To be honest, I have almost no recollection of the caretakers of the schools that I attended.

But from the corner of my kitchen window, I can see him, day and night, watching, caring, and maintaining.

Every day. All day.

Making sure "his" children won't trip over their own carelessness, opening up doors for them, and minding their many needs with pride and quiet diligence.

Observing the unknown caretaker's assiduous work, day in, day out, made me wonder how often we give proper recognition to the sometimes invisible, but nevertheless essential, people in our lives.

Moreover, I wonder, how often do we take a moment to recognize, appreciate, and properly acknowledge and greet the invisible Caretaker of our world?

ᔐ *Take a moment to properly acknowledge all that your Caretaker does for you.*

Because She Is Mine

Barely a week has passed since Sara Leah has entered my life. It's hard to believe how in such a short period of time my world could be so dramatically altered.

It's amazing how this tiny package — less than eight pounds of human being — has made her presence felt throughout my day and night. Every room in our house has been transformed to accommodate her needs. The desk in the family room has become a diaper changing station. Her crib, carriage, rocking seat, and other baby paraphernalia have become the dominant element in our home decor. Hour after hour is taken up with holding her, soothing her, changing her and, of course, the round-the-clock feedings.

The relationship is definitely a give-and-take one. I give her my all, and she takes. She is still a few weeks shy from smiling, cooing back, or even gurgling happily. Most of the time her eyes are shut tight and hold little recognition when they do open. Basically she sleeps, eats, cries, and requires constant care.

But there is nothing that brings me greater contentment than clutching my baby's five perfect tiny fingers or stroking her cottony soft cheeks, her head cradled against my shoulder.

Nor am I the only one in our family to feel this way. All of my children have commented, each in his own way, how much they love "their" baby. How cute, soft, perfect "their" baby sister is — despite the fact that she robs them of their mother's time and attention.

Watching me rocking and singing to Sara Leah for the umpteenth time after a particularly taxing day and grueling night, my husband commented, "It's unbelievable what an outpouring of love a parent shows to her child. Look at what you went through because of her — pregnancy, birth, and then her nonstop crying — yet you still hold her with such adoration."

But this is the love and bond every parent feels toward her newborn. A love simply because she is mine, despite her lack of giving anything back. In fact, it's precisely because she can't give anything in return that the connection is so strong.

Like any parent, I love each of my children unconditionally. But as each of them grows and our relationship deepens, the original pure, unconditional love is no longer as apparent. That bond becomes subsumed within and sidetracked by all that my child gives back to me: the *nachas* (pride), the adorable smiles and hugs, the witty comments, the affection, and the friendship. The more my children grow and mature, the more I no longer only *love* them, but also come to *like* them — as the unique and special personality that each one becomes.

My newborn Sara Leah, however, with her lack of anything to give to me, exemplifies the depth of our simple connection. A pure, intrinsic love deriving wholly from the fact that she is mine.

There is only one thing I can think of that's akin to this love. It is a love that mimics the deep and unconditional love between G-d and us.

It's like the deep bond with G-d that the chassidic masters spoke of: the bond elicited by the simple, spiritually "uncharismatic" individual, who, unlike the spiritually developed tzaddik (righteous individual), gives nothing in return.

Like a parent's love toward her newborn, this strong outpouring of love from G-d to all of us is not due to our merits, talents, or strengths. It's not because of our spiritual stamina or positive qualities or because of any "*nachas*" we may give Him.

It is simply and only because we are His.

❧ *Like the bond of a parent to his child, the bond between you and G-d reflects an outpouring of pure, unconditional love.*

Does G-d Care When I'm Sad?

Recently, at our Institute of Jewish Studies, I organized a mini summer series entitled, "Tears of Joy, Tears of Sorrow."

Several guest speakers examined joy from different vantage points – from a mystical perspective all the way to its psychological side. Rabbis dealt with the spiritual aspects of joy and taught the passages that describe a time of eternal joy. A psychiatrist explained the emotions we experience which plunge us to the depths of the worst feelings of helplessness and provided practical tools to emerge from "pieces to peace."

I had asked a friend of mine to speak on the human-emotional part of this topic. I titled her lecture, "Does G-d Care When I'm Sad?" Rather than the theological or theoretical, she was to touch on the personal core of the human spirit.

I wasn't sure how comfortable my friend would be to open up on a personal level, but I figured that the topic was broad enough to broach more distantly, or, hopefully, more directly. What I was sure of was that this friend had experienced her share of sadness and tragedy. I was positive that she had grappled with this very question many a time.

Though only in her twenties at the time, my friend Esther had fought and overcome two bouts of cancer. As if that wasn't enough, she had lost a child in the most trying of circumstances.

Esther had tucked her two-year-old under his covers one night with a simple case of childhood chickenpox. She awoke the next morning to discover her child dead in his bed. An infection of the blood had fulminated during his sleep, and in the silent, black night the child's organs collapsed, one by one.

At what moment her child closed his eyes for the last time, as well as whether he actually called to his parents, is anyone's guess. But the hard facts of reality confronted Esther in the morning, with the cold body of her child lying before her disbelieving eyes.

Our community was in a state of shock at the abrupt snuffing of this young life. But no one could possibly fathom the immense shock and grief felt by this young mother.

Several years had now passed since that tragic night, and Esther had given birth to several more children. But the trauma of such an immense loss is a wound that never heals entirely. While the pain numbs slightly, the empty hole is carried forever.

My friend began her speech by saying, "While I do not know many of you, I do know why Chana has asked me to speak tonight."

At the outset, Esther asked us, "Please do not mind my tears since this is the first time that I am publicly speaking about such a personal issue. But when Chana called me, I felt that the time had come to confront the challenge and see if I could share."

She explained briefly the events of her child's passing and continued to refer to it as "that night" because it was, understandably, too difficult to enunciate the words "death of my child."

Esther elaborated on the many steps that she went through in coping with her loss. During the first year, it took all of her energy to merely wake up in the morning and get dressed. She described how she had asked my father, her rabbi, while he visited her during shivah (the mourning period immediately following a death), to tell her something — anything, any lesson, any words of comfort. He answered wisely, "No, not now. Now is not yet the time."

By explaining this, Esther validated the need for someone to mourn, to feel the depths of pain, while still blinded by grief, before searching for any understanding.

Esther read for us passages from her personal diary. She showed us, through her entries, her poetry, and her reflections, how she had progressed through the various stages of healing. Incredibly and passionately, she described her deep closeness to G-d throughout her struggles. At times she felt full of questions, anger, depression, and sadness, but, nevertheless, her relationship with Him became far more intense than it had ever been.

With tremendous conviction, she elaborated on her newly achieved awareness and sensitivity as G-d became a real constant in her life.

And then she spoke about her eventual awareness developing and expanding into consideration for others in similar plights. She noted how her own mother had said to her, "My dear daughter, despite the pain you are feeling, you must realize that you do not have a copyright on pain. Others are also in pain and are suffering. Realizing this in no way diminishes your own pain, but rather provides you with the tools for greater sensitivity."

Esther found those tools and that inner strength to address us that evening.

All the lectures in this multipart summer series were interesting, relevant, and informative, but Esther's talk reached a deep place within each of us — precisely because she had spoken straight from her heart, so personally and so honestly.

We grew strong with her courage, we developed newfound faith from her faith, and we cried, silently or openly, along with the tears that streamed down her cheeks.

As I reflected on her talk afterward, I realized that her presentation was the most powerful answer to the ever-present question that plagues us all: Does G-d care when I'm sad?

How can a human being find the strength and courage to emerge from such tragic, personal suffering and still function? Moreover, what provides her with the fortitude to share of her most intimate, personal experiences so that others, too, can learn and grow?

And what pulls people to shed their own indifference and apathy to deeply embrace a stranger's experiences, relive them with her, and become transformed in the process? What opens us up to feeling such enormous sorrow when another human being is sad and such care for another's pain?

Such depths of empathy, caring, and sharing can only be evoked through the power of the G-dly core and connection within each of us.

And, as that G-dly part in each of us surfaced that evening, what was so explicitly revealed — more convincing than any argument could be — was that we care, simply and only, because You, G-d, care.

❧ *Our uniqueness as human beings emerges when the G-dly core in each of us surfaces.*

These journal questions reflect values from the stories you just read. Record your answers for a greater awareness of your spiritual perspective on life.

On Finding G-d
JOURNAL

1. What role does G-d play in your life?

2. Describe a situation in your life when you felt a deep connection and bond with G-d.

3. Describe a situation in your life when you felt like G-d was "hiding." What steps did you take to feel more connected?

4. Take a moment today to acknowledge the good that G-d does for you.

5. Do you feel hopeful or resigned for the world?

Glossary

bar mitzvah — A celebration marking the thirteenth year of a boy's life, the age when he is considered mature and obligated in the commandments. (A girl's celebration is called a bat mitzvah, celebrated at twelve years.)

beit midrash — Study hall where adult males study Torah, usually in pairs.

bentch — To bless.

bikur cholim — Visiting the sick; a volunteer organization that provides aid to the sick or their families.

bitachon — Trust in G-d.

brit milah — Circumcision performed when a baby boy is eight days old as prescribed in the Torah (Genesis 17).

bubby — Grandmother.

chassidim — Members of the movement started by Rabbi Israel Ba'al Shem Tov (1698–1760) stressing the service of G-d with love, joy, and meticulous observance of the mitzvot.

Chassidut — The teachings of the masters of the chassidic movement.

chevrah kaddisha — The society responsible for the burial of, and performing the rites on, the dead.

daven — Pray.

Elul — The twelfth and last of the Jewish months immediately preceding the High Holidays.

emunah — Faith in G-d.

farbrengen — A chassidic gathering punctuated with words of Torah, stories, and heartwarming songs.

galut — Exile; the exile of the Jewish people, which began from the time of the destruction of the First Temple in 423 BCE and will end when the Messiah arrives.

hachnasat orchim — Hospitality extended to guests.

halachah — Jewish law.

Hashem — Literally, "the Name"; a reference to G-d.

hei — The fifth letter of the Hebrew alphabet, pronounced like the letter H.

hekdesh — The part of a Jewish cemetery designated for the burial of society's outcasts or destitute.

kapparot — A ritual performed on the eve of Yom Kippur where a prayer is said under a live chicken (or fish) asking G-d to accept the death of the animal in lieu of our own.

keruvim — The cherubim, two angelic forms which were part of the covering of the Ark which housed the original Tablets that Moses brought down from Sinai. The Ark was kept in the holiest part of the Temple.

Kotel — Literally, "the wall," referring to the western retaining wall of the Temple Mount in Jerusalem. The wall dates back to the second Temple period and its proximity to the Temple Mount makes it the holiest place where Jews can pray in our times.

l'chaim — Literally, "to life"; said as a toast to life over a cup of wine or spirits.

mazal tov — Literally, "good luck"; said to convey congratulations for any happy occasion or celebration.

menorah — Candelabra; an eight-branched *menorah* is lit in Jewish homes on the festival of Hanukkah.

Minyan — A prayer quorum made up of a minimum of ten men.

mitzvah (pl. *mitzvot*) — Commandment from G-d.

nachas — Jewish pride and pleasure, especially from one's children.

ohel — The grave site of a holy individual.

Pesach — Passover, the holiday commemorating the Jewish people's exodus from Egypt in 1313 BCE.

pikuach nefesh — Life-threatening.

parashah — Torah portion. The Bible is divided into fifty-three of these sections, read each week and completed each year.

Rebbetzin — A rabbi's wife.

roshei yeshivah — Dean of a Torah academy.

Savta — Grandmother.

sefarim — Books of Torah.

sefer Torah — A handwritten Torah scroll containing all five books of Moses.

Shabbaton — A special gathering or convention held over a Sabbath weekend.

Shabbat — Sabbath; the seventh day of the week, celebrated as a day of rest and spiritual focus as prescribed in the Torah (Exodus 20).

shalom aleichem — Words of greeting meaning "peace be with you."

Shechinah — The presence of G-d in our world.

Shema — The most important declaration of our belief in the Oneness of G-d (from Deuteronomy 6).

shivah — The seven-day mourning period immediately following the death of a close family member.

shul — Synagogue.

Tehillim — The book of Psalms composed by King David and recited in times of thanksgiving as well as in trying times.

Tishrei — The first month of the Jewish calendar marking the beginning of the year. This month begins with the High Holidays.

Torah — Literally the five books of Moses, but generally referring to the whole body of Jewish law and teachings.

tzaddikim — Individuals of unique holiness and saintliness.

tzaros — Suffering.

vidui — Prayer of confession.

Yaakov — Jacob, the third and last forefather of the Jewish people.

yeshivah — Academy of higher Torah learning.

Yiddishkeit — Judaism.

yud — The tenth letter of the Hebrew alphabet, pronounced like a Y.

Zeidy — Grandfather.

About the Author

Chana Weisberg lectures worldwide on a wide array of issues relating to women, relationships, the soul, faith, and mysticism.

She is the author of *The Crown of Creation: The Lives of Great Biblical Women based on Rabbinical and Mystical Sources* (Oakville, Canada: Mosaic Press, 1996) and *The Feminine Soul: A Mystical Journey Exploring the Essence of Feminine Spirituality* (Toronto: Jacobson and Davidson, 2001).

Chana Weisberg has also published three resource textbooks as part of a Feminine Voices Series based on her first book, *The Crown of Creation*. Her next book, *Jewish Women: Past, Present, and Future*, is soon to be released.

Chana Weisberg serves as the dean of the Jewish Russian Community Center's Institute of Jewish Studies in Toronto, which offers comprehensive educational courses and outreach programs for men and women of all backgrounds. She is also a regular columnist for *The Jewish Press*, the largest Anglo-Jewish newspaper, as well as www.chabad.org *Weekly Magazine*. Her articles appear regularly on Aish.com and other Jewish mediums. She also serves as one of the resident scholars of www. askmoses.com.

Chana descends from a long line of distinguished rabbis and resides with her husband, Rabbi Isser Zalman Weisberg, and their six children in Toronto, Canada.